CREPES
THE FINE ART OF CREPE AND BLINTZ COOKING

PUBLISHER: R. ARTHUR BARRETT
EDITOR: CAROL D. BRENT
PHOTOGAPHY: BILL MILLER

Book Trade Distribution by
DOUBLEDAY & COMPANY, INC.
Garden City, New York

TESTED RECIPE PUBLISHERS, INC. CHICAGO
A DIVISION OF JOHN BLAIR & COMPANY

CONTENTS

FIRST PRINTING—AUGUST 1976

ISBN 0-385-12801-0 Doubleday
ISBN 0-88351-007-3 T.R.P.
Library of Congress Catalog Card Number 76-25350

A DIVISION OF JOHN BLAIR & COMPANY

INTRODUCTION

Say "crepe" and people immediately think of fancy restaurants, elegant sauces with French names, and super sophisticated meals.

But what is a crepe? Nothing more, really, than a slender, tender pancake. Although the French get credit for crepes, since the name is French, many other countries, all around the world, have long used an egg-flour-milk pancake to embrace as astounding variety of foods.

Long regarded as a fancy restaurant dish, the crepe, like so many other now-classy specialties, is a practical, peasant-created food, probably mothered by that greatest of all motivators—necessity. The crepe is in many ways like a sandwich, or an omelet—it can hold almost anything, and make its contents a meal.

The word *crepe* can refer to the pancake itself, or the filled, topped or sauced pancake. How you pronounce it is really up to you, since the French word has, through popular usage, become quite Americanized. The French write the word *crêpe* and say it krep, as in step. Americans seem to be more comfortable with just plain *crepe,* said as in shape or drape.

In addition to elegance and flavor, crepes are just plain good food. Eggs, milk and enriched flour—the basic ingredients—are an important part of a day's wise eating plan. Adding meat, poultry, fish or more eggs, fruits and vegetables just helps you round out a meal.

ALL ABOUT CREPES

CREPE PANS

Not so many years ago the only crepe pan you could find was a small skillet with sloped, flaring sides. Now there's a dizzying array of pans on the market, quite different in appearance and in style, but all designed for cooking crepes.

TRADITIONAL PANS
FOR COOKING CREPES

The traditional crepe or omelet pan, a slope- or flare-sided skillet anywhere from 5½ to 8 inches across the bottom, still makes very good crepes, although the crepes are slightly thicker than those baked on dip pans. Traditional crepe pans come in stainless steel, copper with tin linings, enamel over iron, cast iron or aluminum. Some have non-stick linings, others don't. Purists insist that crepe or omelet pans should be reserved for crepes or omelets only, but if your storage space or budget is limited, a single skillet can perform too many tasks to be kept only for a few uses. If you have used your crepe pan for other cooking, wipe it out with a mixture of 1 teaspoon salt and 1 tablespoon oil. Wipe with paper towels and it's ready to go again.

Always follow the seasoning directions that come with your pan—you'll be rewarded with better performance. If no seasoning directions came with your pan and it does not have a non-stick finish, wash pan well in hot suds, rinse and dry. Spread inside of pan with shortening or oil and put pan on low heat for about 15 minutes or until pan is hot. Remove from heat, let cool and then wipe oil from pan with paper towel. Repeat oiling and heating one more time.

Do remember that well-seasoned crepe pans mustn't be washed in detergent, or you'll lose the seasoning. Just wipe out with a paper towel after using.

Dip pans, or bottom-bakers, were the logical result of a search for a method that could produce the thinnest crepes possible. These pans usually have a dome or slightly rounded shape, and the batter cooks on the outside of the pan. You preheat the pan, dip the dome side quickly into the batter, then invert the pan over heating element to cook. Some of these dip pans have non-stick coatings, and some require special seasoning, so follow the manufacturer's directions. The most expensive of these pans aren't always the best, so shop wisely. One manufacturer has created a standard-looking skillet that lets you cook inside or on the bottom.

Electric crepe pans provide controlled, even heat, so important for perfect cooking and browning of crepes. Most electric pans are dip pans or bottom bakers, but one is a small, round electric skillet with a special non-stick coating. The electrics have non-stick finishes for easy removal of crepes and for easy care. Look for an electric pan that is lightweight, easy to handle, and cool to handle. Electric crepe pans are, obviously, more expensive than skillets or most top of the range pans.

Other pans include a small, flat, very shallow non-stick lined pan that allows you to pour off excess batter so crepes will be thin.

A cast iron crepe pan works top of range, and has a "moat" to catch excess batter, so crepes will be even and thin.

Crepe Equipment

There are other kitchen helpers, in addition to pans, that can simplify crepe cooking and serving.

FINISHING PAN, or Crepe Suzette Pan. This pan is large, usually round, always shallow and often copper. It is designed for elegant presentation of crepes at the table. Crepes "finished" in these pans are usually the quarter-folded crepes in a fruit sauce or syrup for dessert. You often see finishing pans used in restaurants that specialize in flaming foods. You could use a finishing pan over a home-size portable burner, canned heat or over the heating unit of your chafing dish.

FINISHING PAN
OR CREPE SUZETTE PAN

CHAFING DISH. The blazer or top pan of a chafing dish can be an impressive way to present crepes, especially for dessert. You could also bring main dish crepes to the table, but it might be difficult to arrange that many filled and rolled crepes in a single pan.

ELECTRIC SKILLET. A very practical and easy way to present crepes at the table is in your electric skillet. That way you can keep extra servings warm. Use a low heat setting.

BAKING DISHES OR PANS. Most main dish crepes are best filled, rolled or folded and then arranged in a greased shallow baking pan, dish or casserole, then heated in the oven. The recipes in this book suggest 13 x 9 x 2-inch baking pans or dishes, since standard crepes fit easily into that size pan. But if you have a favorite earthenware, enamel or metal casserole or serving dish that approximates that size, by all means use it. Don't forget that there are basket or pretty metal holders for standard sized baking dishes and pans, so they can come right from oven to table.

TOOLS. A small spatula can be a great help in removing crepes from pan, in spreading filling or turning edges of crepe over as you begin to roll or fold.

A pancake turner and a pretty server with a long narrow blade will help serve crepes from baking pan.

Measuring cups, a nested set, are important for preparing batters and fillings, but are also very important for portioning out amounts of batter for baking and filling. The recipes give you the approximate measure of filling to be put on each crepe, so you come out even at the end of the filling and the end of the crepes. You can usually measure out what 1 portion will look like, then gauge the rest by spooning it onto crepes.

BAKERS. Cooks who make and serve a lot of crepes have discovered the joy of individual bakers, much like those used in many creperies. These oval, ovenproof dishes can hold a filled crepe, or two, or three, for its trip to oven or broiler and then right to the table.

Crepe Sizes

Most crepe pans produce crepes that range from 5½ inches in diameter to about 8 inches in diameter. For some recipes the size of the crepe is unimportant. But in some recipes a crepe size is given, because the amount of filling is designed to be held by so many crepes of a particular size. The recipes that follow call for small crepes in the 5½ to 6-inch range, large crepes as 6½ to 7-inch. If your crepe pan produces small crepes and the recipe calls for 7-inchers, just bake more crepes and use less filling in each. If your pan produces large crepes and the recipe calls for 5½ to 6-inch crepes, you'll use less crepes with more filling in each.

How To Bake Crepes

Traditional Pans. Season pan, if new. Heat pan until a drop of water skitters. If water vaporizes immediately, pan is too hot. If water doesn't move at all, pan isn't hot enough. When pan is just right, add a teaspoon of butter and melt, if pan does not have non-stick coating.

Pour in batter, Fig. 1, tip and twirl pan so batter completely covers bottom of pan.

Figure 1

5

The trick is to discover exactly how much batter this takes, Fig. 2, and then to add that amount each time. A few trials will show you.

Figure 2

The batter should begin to set immediately, Fig. 3. Medium to medium-high heat seems best for most crepe baking, but the exact setting is something you have to work out with your range.

Figure 3

When crepe is dry on top and edges begin to brown, Fig. 4, loosen edge with spatula or turner.

Figure 4

Turn crepes with a flip of the wrist, Fig. 5 and brown other side, if you wish. It isn't necessary to brown crepes on both sides because filling usually goes on the unbrowned side.

Figure 5

Heating Filled Crepes

Filled crepes can be served immediately, or heated in the oven. It's best to arrange filled crepes in a greased baking dish, pan or casserole. If filling isn't too runny or there isn't a sauce topping you can heat crepes on greased baking sheet or jelly roll pan.

Twenty to thirty minutes at 350°F. or 375°F. will get most crepes piping hot. If you've prepared crepes several hours in advance and refrigerated them, add another 5 to 10 minutes to the baking time. It isn't necessary to cover crepes during baking. Some cooks do prefer to cover crepes with foil. If covered, crepes don't brown. If uncovered they will brown slightly.

Crepes that are topped with sauce, cheese or crumbs can be heated in a quick trip under the broiler. Broiling also melts the cheese, browns the crumbs or gives a nice glaze to sauce toppings. Preheat the broiler, arrange crepes on or in a greased shallow pan and broil 3 to 5 inches from heat just until topping is bubbly or melts. Watch carefully because uncovered crepes can brown very quickly. Crepes can also be heated in just minutes in the microwave oven. Follow your microwave manufacturer's direction for time suggestions.

Non-Electric Dip Pans. Always follow instructions that come with your particular model pan for seasoning, preheating and dipping. Some dip pans require special seasoning, others have non-stick finish. Pour batter into deep dinner plate, pie plate or pan or other similar container. Put pan on heating element on range and heat over medium to medium-high heat until pan is hot enough to sizzle a drop of water. Water should skitter on the surface of the pan. If it vaporizes immediately pan is too hot. If water doesn't move at all, pan isn't hot enough.

Dip heated pan quickly into batter, Fig. 1, tilting and tipping slightly so entire surface of pan is coated with batter. A trial crepe or two will help you determine just which heat setting on your range is best for the particular pan, and for the particular batter, you're using. Hold pan above pan of batter for just a second or two, so excess batter can run off.

Figure 1

Then invert pan on heating element Fig. 2, and cook until crepe is dry on top and browning slightly around edges.

Figure 2

Remove pan from heat, loosen edge of crepe with knife or spatula, Fig. 3, then invert pan over plate or waxed paper. Depending on pan, crepe may peel or fall off on its own, or may need some assistance from you in peeling off.

Figure 3

Handling Baked Crepes

If you are going to fill crepes right away, stack them as they are baked and keep warm in a 250°F. oven. Crepes must be covered with a sheet of foil or they will dry out. Crepes will separate easily if you put a square of waxed paper between each crepe as you stack them.

Or you can stack crepes, as you bake them, in a deep plate or pie pan or plate. Keep covered with foil or pan lid so they stay flexible and hot.

Freezing Filled Crepes

Many filled crepes can be successfully frozen. If in doubt as to whether a filling will freeze successfully or not, remember that very saucy fillings may separate slightly upon reheating, hard-cooked egg whites may toughen, mayonnaise will separate and fruits and vegetables may change texture slightly.

Wrap filled crepes closely in plastic wrap or foil and seal. Thaw several hours in the refrigerator or unwrap and put into oven without thawing, adding 15 to 20 minutes to heating time given in recipe. Reheat in microwave oven, following manufacturer's directions.

Figure 1

Figure 2

Figure 3

8

Electric Dip Pans. Always follow the instructions that come with your particular model pan for seasoning, preheating and dipping. The instructions here are general, for all electric dip pans. Pour batter into a deep dinner plate, pie plate or pan or other similar container.

Dip heated pan into batter, Fig. 1, being sure to tip and tilt pan slightly in batter so entire surface of pan is coated. Do not hold pan in batter for too long, or crepe will immediately form and then slip off into batter. A second or two dip is really all that's necessary. After a trial or two you will be able to judge exactly.

Hold pan up above pan of batter for just a second so excess batter can drip off, then quickly invert and set pan on its feet, Fig. 2, or heating base to cook the crepe. Instructions will tell you how to judge doneness for each particular brand of crepe pan, but usually you can see the crepe is dry on the top and beginning to brown around the edges.

Loosen crepe around edges, Fig. 3, following manufacturer's instructions, then invert pan over plate or waxed paper and let crepe peel or fall off.

Freezing Crepes

Because crepes keep so well in the freezer it's often a good idea to make up an extra batch or two to bake. The freezer can hold them at the ready for planned or unplanned meals.

Bake crepes as usual and let them cool. Stack with waxed paper between each crepe. Wrap in several thicknesses of plastic wrap and seal. Or wrap in foil and seal. Or put in heavy-duty plastic bag and tie or seal. Crepes must be well-covered and air tight or they will dry out.

Put wrapped crepes in flat area of freezer. They will keep for several weeks.

TO THAW: Remove crepes from freezer and let stand at room temperature about an hour. After about 15 minutes at room temperature you should be able to separate individual crepes (if there's waxed paper in between) and they'll thaw faster. You can also thaw crepes in a 250°F. oven, separating and turning so they don't dry out, or thaw in microwave oven for just a few seconds, following manufacturer's directions for thawing.

Figure 1

Figure 2

Figure 3

Figure 4 ▲

▼ Figure 5

Filling Crepes

For most recipes it is easiest to spoon required amount of filling down the center of each crepe. Fillings that are smooth can be spread over the entire crepe. Use a measuring cup to portion out filling onto first crepe. Then you can judge about how much to spoon or spread on remaining crepes. Portioning this way lets you fill, roll or fold one crepe at a time and put in baking pan, saving you from spreading all crepes out on the counter.

Folding Crepes

Rolling crepes is one of the easiest ways of capturing filling inside. Either spoon filling down center or spread over inner circle of crepe.

Starting at any side, Fig. 1, roll crepe up like jelly roll.

Bring far end of crepe over top, Fig. 2, to complete roll. Place rolled crepe in dish with seam side down, so filling will stay in place.

Folding crepes in quarters is an easy and attractive variation. Just spread filling over inner circle of crepe, or portion filling onto 1 quarter of crepe.

Fold crepe in half, Fig. 3, with edge almost meeting.

Fold halved crepe in half again, Fig. 4, with edges meeting.

Quarter-folded crepes are often used for Suzette or other fruit fillings.

As a further variation on the quarter-fold, push sides of folded crepe in to form flower-like shape, Fig. 5. This is also a handy way to shape crepes to fit into muffin cups.

Refrigerating Crepes

Unfilled crepes can be stacked, wrapped and refrigerated for several days.

Crepe batter will keep up to a week in the refrigerator, if properly covered. Stir batter before using, and add a tablespoon or two of milk if it has become too thick.

Crepe batter can be frozen, but it takes so long to thaw that it's really simpler just to mix up a new batch.

CREPE BATTERS

Crepe batter has only a few ingredients: eggs, milk or water, flour, melted butter or oil, and a little salt. But the proportions of these ingredients are very important. Too much or too little of any one and the batter will be too thick or too thin, will stick to the pan or won't set.

The recipes that follow have just the right proportions of ingredients to guarantee success. They have all been tested on traditional crepe pans and electric and top-of-range dip pans.

It often takes one or two tries to get the hang of crepe baking, working out the exact temperature and the proper consistency of the batter. Fortunately your losses—a crepe or two—will be minimal and inexpensive. Even experienced crepe cooks figure that the first crepe out is a trial run, every time. And, even if it takes you more than a few trials before you've got the knack, crepe batter is very easy to mix up.

Crepe batter can be mixed up by hand, with a rotary or electric mixer, with a whisk or, simplest of all, in the blender. Most crepe recipes direct you to refrigerate batter for about an hour before baking. This allows the foam incorporated during mixing to disappear and, more importantly, gives the flour time to absorb some of the liquid. This may mean that batter becomes a little thicker after standing than it was when you mixed it. The proper consistency of almost every crepe batter is like thick cream. Feel free to add a tablespoon of flour, if batter seems too thin, or a tablespoon of milk if it seems too thick. Adding more than that shouldn't be necessary.

Some crepe cooks feel they get the very best crepes if they mix up the batter several hours, even a day or two, in advance and then let it stand at room temperature for 15 to 20 minutes before baking. This is fine, if you've planned that far ahead.

If you decide on the spur of the moment to have some crepes, it's perfectly all right to mix up batter and bake it right away.

BATTER YIELDS:

The exact number of crepes you will get from any particular batter depends on the consistency of the batter, the type of pan you are using and the size of the pan you are using. Small (5½ to 6-inch) traditional crepe pans require about 2 tablespoons of batter for each crepe. Large traditional pans (7½ to 8-inches) will take almost ¼ cup per crepe. Dip pans take about 3 tablespoons for each large crepe, but the exact amount depends very much on the pan itself—its size, shape and temperature.

Basic Dessert Crepe Batter

A basic sweet batter which can easily be varied to suit its filling.

3 eggs
½ cup milk
½ cup water
3 tablespoons butter, melted
1 cup all-purpose flour
1 to 2 tablespoons sugar
¼ teaspoon salt

BLENDER METHOD: Combine all ingredients in blender container. Blend about 1 minute. Scrape down sides of blender container with rubber spatula. Blend until smooth, about 30 additional seconds.

MIXER, ROTARY BEATER OR WHISK METHOD: Combine eggs, milk, water and butter in mixing bowl. Beat until combined. Add flour, sugar and salt. Beat until smooth.

Refrigerate batter 1 hour.
YIELD: About 2 cups batter.

VARIATIONS:

EXTRACT-FLAVORED: Use 1 tablespoon sugar. Add ½ teaspoon of desired flavor extract to batter.

LEMON: Use 2 tablespoons sugar. Add 2 teaspoons grated lemon peel to batter.

TIPSY: Use 1 tablespoon sugar. Add 1 tablespoon brandy or favorite liqueur to batter.

Corn Meal Crepe Batter

A hearty crepe, good for Mexican fillings or breakfast dishes.

3 eggs
½ cup milk
½ cup chicken broth or water
3 tablespoons butter, melted
1 cup corn meal
¼ teaspoon salt

BLENDER METHOD: Combine all ingredients in blender container. Blend about 1 minute. Scrape down sides of blender container with rubber spatula. Blend until well combined, about 30 additional seconds.

MIXER, ROTARY BEATER OR WHISK METHOD: Combine eggs, milk, broth and butter in mixing bowl. Beat until combined. Add corn meal and salt; beat until combined.

Refrigerate batter 1 hour. Batter must be stirred between each crepe as corn meal will sink. Loosen with pancake turner or spatula to remove from pan.

YIELD: about 2 cups batter.

VARIATION: For a lighter corn meal crepe, substitute ½ cup all-purpose flour for ½ cup of the corn meal.

Cocoa Crepe Batter

A tasty dessert crepe batter chocolate lovers will appreciate.

3 eggs
1 cup buttermilk
2 tablespoons butter, melted
¾ cup all-purpose flour
3 tablespoons cocoa
3 tablespoons sugar

BLENDER METHOD: Combine all ingredients in blender container. Blend about 1 minute. Scrape down sides of blender container with rubber spatula. Blend until smooth, about 30 additional seconds.

MIXER, ROTARY BEATER OR WHISK METHOD: Combine eggs, buttermilk and butter in mixing bowl. Beat until combined. Add flour, cocoa and sugar. Beat until smooth.

Refrigerate batter 1 hour.

YIELD: about 2¼ cups batter.

NOTE: If buttermilk is not available, add milk to 1 tablespoon vinegar or lemon juice to make 1 cup.

Basic Crepe Batter

An easy to remember batter with many variations (see below) that works on regular, electric or bottom-baking crepe pans.

1½ cups milk
3 eggs
2 tablespoons butter, melted
1 cup all-purpose flour
½ teaspoon salt

BLENDER METHOD: Combine all ingredients in blender container. Blend about 1 minute. Scrape down sides of blender container with rubber spatula. Blend until well combined, about 30 additional seconds.

MIXER, ROTARY BEATER OR WHISK METHOD: Combine milk, eggs and butter in mixing bowl. Beat until combined. Add flour and salt. Beat until smooth.

Refrigerate batter 1 hour before baking. Stir batter before baking.

YIELD: about 3 cups batter.

VANILLA CREPES: Add 1 to 2 teaspoons vanilla extract and 1 tablespoon sugar to Basic Crepe Batter.

WHOLE WHEAT CREPES: Replace ½ cup of the all-purpose flour with whole wheat flour. Be sure to stir batter between each crepe, or whole wheat flour will sink.

RYE CARAWAY CREPES: Replace ½ cup of the all-purpose flour in Basic Crepe Batter with ½ cup rye flour. Add 1 teaspoon caraway seed.

ORANGE DESSERT CREPES: Add 1 tablespoon sugar and 2 teaspoons grated orange peel to Basic Crepe Batter.

OATMEAL CREPES: Add 1 envelope instant plain oatmeal to Basic Crepe Batter.

PARMESAN CREPES: Add ¼ cup grated Parmesan cheese to Basic Crepe Batter.

HERBED CREPES: Add ½ teaspoon crushed dried basil, oregano, savory or dill weed to Basic Crepe Batter.

Try Yogurt Crepe Batter and Dieter's Crepe Batter on Page 81.

Macaroon Dessert Crepe Batter

For a very easy dessert, just wrap these crepes around a dip of ice cream and spoon some sundae sauce over. This batter works well in (or on) all crepe pans and makers.

2 eggs
1 cup milk
¼ cup light cream or half and half
1 tablespoon butter, melted
⅓ cup macaroon crumbs
1 cup all-purpose flour
2 tablespoons sugar
Dash salt

BLENDER METHOD: Combine all ingredients in blender container. Blend about 1 minute. Scrape down sides of blender container with rubber spatula. Blend until well combined, about 30 additional seconds.

MIXER, ROTARY BEATER OR WHISK METHOD: Combine eggs, milk, cream and butter in mixing bowl. Add macaroon crumbs, flour, sugar and salt and beat until smooth.

Refrigerate batter 1 hour.

YIELD: About 2 cups batter.

Chocolate Crepe Batter

1 package (6 oz.) semi-sweet chocolate morsels
3 tablespoons butter
4 eggs
½ cup milk
½ cup water
1 tablespoon vanilla extract
1 cup all-purpose flour
1 cup sifted powdered sugar
1 teaspoon salt

Melt chocolate and butter together over very low heat. Remove from heat and cool slightly.

BLENDER METHOD: Combine all ingredients in blender container. Blend about 1 minute. Scrape down sides of blender container with rubber spatula. Blend until well combined, about 30 additional seconds.

MIXER, ROTARY BEATER OR WHISK METHOD: Combine eggs, milk, water, vanilla and chocolate mixture in mixing bowl. Beat until combined. Add flour, sugar and salt. Beat until smooth.

Refrigerate batter 1 hour.

YIELD: About 3½ cups batter.

Souffle Crepes

Serve these "as is" or top with fruit and whipped cream. This batter is just as delightful in Pineapple Puffs.

1 cup all-purpose flour
⅔ cup granulated sugar
6 eggs, separated
⅓ cup butter, melted
1 cup milk
¼ teaspoon grated lemon peel or cream of tartar
Powdered sugar

Combine flour and granulated sugar in mixing bowl; add egg yolks and butter. Beat on low speed until mixture is a smooth, thick paste, about 3 to 5 minutes. Add milk; beat until combined. Wash beaters. Beat egg whites and lemon peel until stiff but not dry or just until whites no longer slip when bowl is tilted. Gently fold yolk mixture into whites. Cook on both sides, using ¼ cup batter for each crepe. Dust with powdered sugar while hot. Keep cooked crepes warm in 200°F. oven while completing crepe cooking. To serve: Cut into wedges. YIELD: 24 (5-inch) crepes or 4 to 6 servings.

NOTE: Recommended for traditional crepe pans only.

Hungarian Crepe Batter (Palacsinta)

Almost like the basic crepes. If you wish, for dessert recipes, add 2 tablespoons sugar to the batter.

3 eggs
1 cup milk
2 tablespoons butter, melted
1 cup all-purpose flour
¾ teaspoon salt

BLENDER METHOD: Combine all ingredients in blender container. Blend about 1 minute. Scrape down sides of blender container with rubber spatula. Blend until well combined, about 30 additional seconds.

MIXER, ROTARY BEATER OR WHISK METHOD: Combine eggs, milk and butter in mixing bowl. Beat until combined. Add flour and salt. Beat until smooth.

Refrigerate batter 1 hour.

YIELD: About 2¼ cups batter.

Dessert Crepe Batter

3 eggs
1 cup milk
¼ cup light cream or half and half
1½ tablespoons brandy
1½ tablespoons butter, melted
1 cup all-purpose flour
¼ cup sugar
Dash salt

BLENDER METHOD: Combine all ingredients in blender container. Blend about 1 minute. Scrape down sides of blender container with rubber spatula. Blend until smooth, about 30 additional seconds.

MIXER, ROTARY BEATER OR WHISK METHOD: Combine eggs, milk, cream, brandy and butter in mixing bowl. Beat until combined. Add flour, sugar and salt. Beat until smooth.

Refrigerate batter 1 hour.

YIELD: about 3 cups batter.

Biscuit Mix Crepe Batter

1 cup packaged all-purpose biscuit mix
3 eggs
¾ cup milk

BLENDER METHOD: Combine all ingredients in blender container. Blend about 1 minute. Scrape down sides of blender container with rubber spatula. Blend until smooth, about 30 additional seconds.

MIXER, ROTARY BEATER OR WHISK METHOD: Combine all ingredients in bowl and beat until smooth.

Refrigerate batter 1 hour.

YIELD: about 1⅞ cups batter.

Pancake Mix Crepe Batter

3 eggs
¾ cup milk
¾ cup pancake mix

BLENDER METHOD: Combine all ingredients in blender container. Blend about 1 minute. Scrape down sides of blender container with rubber spatula. Blend until well combined, about 30 additional seconds.

MIXER, ROTARY BEATER OR WHISK METHOD: Combine all ingredients in mixing bowl. Beat until combined. Refrigerate 1 hour.

YIELD: About 1¾ cups batter.

Sour Cream Crepe Batter

This batter is a little richer and thicker than the Basic Batters and makes crepes that are slightly thicker.

3 eggs
¾ cup light cream or half and half
½ cup dairy sour cream
3 tablespoons butter, melted
1 cup all-purpose flour
3 tablespoons sugar
Dash salt

BLENDER METHOD: Combine all ingredients in blender container. Blend about 1 minute. Scrape down sides of blender container with rubber spatula. Blend until well combined, about 30 additional seconds.

MIXER, ROTARY BEATER OR WHISK METHOD: Combine eggs, cream, sour cream and butter in mixing bowl. Beat until combined. Add flour, sugar and salt. Beat until smooth.

Refrigerate batter 1 hour. YIELD: about 2½ cups batter.

Graham Dessert Crepe Batter

A delightful crepe batter for a change of pace.

3 eggs
½ cup milk
½ cup water
3 tablespoons butter, melted
½ cup graham cracker crumbs (about 6 square crackers)
½ cup all-purpose flour
1 tablespoon sugar
¼ teaspoon salt

BLENDER METHOD: Combine all ingredients in blender container; blend about 1 minute. Scrape down sides of blender container with rubber spatula. Blend until smooth, about 30 additional seconds.

MIXER, ROTARY BEATER OR WHISK METHOD: Combine eggs, milk, water and butter in mixing bowl; beat until combined. Add cracker crumbs, flour, sugar and salt; beat until smooth.

Refrigerate batter 1 hour.

YIELD: about 2¼ cups batter.

A

B

C

APPETIZER CREPES

Crepes make magnificent appetizers! You can spread almost any prepared dip, cheese spread, or any spreadable mixture, over crepes, roll them up and let them chill hours in advance of your party.

Or fill crepes with savory hot fillings and keep them hot in a chafing dish or on a warming tray on your buffet.

Remember that almost any mixture you can spread or spoon can go into a crepe. And don't forget to try spreading crepe layers and then stacking them high for an impressive gateau or cake. You can also halve crepes to make finger-size or one or two bite servings, wrapping them around or folding them over fillings.

Try using a variety of batter flavorings along with the filling recipes that follow. Parmesan batter adds a delicate fragrance and flavor to many fillings; whole wheat and corn meal crepes have unique flavor and texture.

With crepes on hand in your freezer you can have a tray full of appetizers at almost a moment's notice, and put on a party with the greatest of ease.

Shrimp Rolls

See photo at left.

Quick, easy and ever so tangy! Great for a cocktail party.

12 (5½ to 6-inch) Crepes
3 tablespoons butter, softened
½ cup grated Parmesan cheese
1 egg, slightly beaten
2 tablespoons sherry
½ teaspoon Worcestershire sauce
⅛ teaspoon cayenne pepper
½ lb. small shrimp, cleaned, cooked and drained

Beat butter, cheese, egg, sherry, Worcestershire sauce and cayenne until well combined. Stir in shrimp. Spoon about 2 tablespoons mixture down center of each crepe. Fold 1 side up to cover filling; tuck ends in. Complete rolling with remaining side. Place on baking sheet. Bake in preheated 425°F. oven 5 minutes.   YIELD: 12 appetizers.
NOTE: Refrigerate any leftovers.

Mushroom Crepe Quiches

See photo at left.

An appetizer to please most any palate. Provide forks so your guests can savor every morsel.

12 (5½ to 6-inch) Crepes
¼ cup butter
½ cup chopped onion
½ lb. fresh mushrooms, sliced
½ cup shredded Swiss cheese
4 eggs
1 cup whipping cream, light cream or half and half
½ teaspoon salt
Dash cayenne pepper

In skillet melt butter. Add onion and saute until tender but not brown, about 3 minutes. Add mushrooms; cook an additional 5 minutes. Remove from heat. The greased 3-inch muffin cups with crepes, being careful not to puncture crepes. Place about 2 tablespoons mushroom mixture in each crepe-lined cup. Sprinkle each with 2 teaspoons cheese. Beat together eggs, cream and seasonings. Pour 3 tablespoons egg mixture into each cup over cheese. Bake in preheated 375°F. oven 25 to 30 minutes or until knife inserted near center comes out clean. Let stand 5 minutes before serving.   YIELD: 12 appetizers.
NOTE: Refrigerate any leftovers.

Peanut-Chutney Appetizer Crepes

Use crunchy peanut butter for extra texture.

24 (5½ to 6-inch) Crepes
1 cup crunchy peanut butter
1 cup chopped chutney
¼ cup minced celery

Blend peanut butter, chutney and celery. Spread about 1½ tablespoons on each crepe. Roll up and cut in half to serve. YIELD: 48 appetizers.

Party Pate Crepelettes

Very tasty in herb crepes. A make-ahead recipe to make entertaining easy.

12 (6½ to 7-inch) Crepes
⅓ cup butter
1 cup finely chopped onion
1 lb. chicken livers
2 hard-cooked eggs, finely chopped
2 tablespoons brandy or cognac
1 teaspoon salt
1 teaspoon thyme
½ teaspoon marjoram, crushed
Dash pepper
24 slices bacon, halved

In skillet melt butter; add onion and saute until tender but not brown, about 3 minutes. Remove to mixing bowl with slotted spoon. Cook livers in remaining butter until tender, stirring to cook both sides, about 5 to 10 minutes. Mince or grind livers. Add to onions along with eggs, brandy and seasonings. Mix well. Spread about ¼ cup mixture over each crepe. Roll tightly. Chill until firm. To serve: Cut each crepe roll into quarters. Wrap with ½ slice bacon and fasten with wooden picks. Broil 6 inches from heat 5 to 10 minutes or until bacon is crisp. Serve hot. YIELD: 48 appetizers.

Scallop Crepe Roll-ups

An appetizer that you can prepare in advance. Chopped shrimp or tuna would be a tasty substitute for scallops.

12 (6½ to 7-inch) Crepes
1 package (12 oz.) frozen scallops
1 cup dairy sour cream
½ cup mayonnaise or salad dressing
¼ cup grated Parmesan cheese
2 tablespoons sliced pitted ripe olives
2 tablespoons sliced green onion

Cook scallops according to package directions; drain and chop. Blend sour cream, mayonnaise and Parmesan, then stir in olives, green onion and scallops. Spread about 3 tablespoons filling over each crepe. Roll up. Chill until serving time. YIELD: 12 servings.

Chili Crab Crepes

These appetizers are nice to serve from a buffet. They also make an excellent first course for a formal meal.

12 (6½ to 7-inch) Crepes
1 cup dairy sour cream
1 package (3 oz.) cream cheese, softened
1 tablespoon *each* finely chopped green
  pepper, parsley, and onion
1 tablespoon prepared horseradish
1 tablespoon lemon juice
1 tablespoon olive oil
1 can (about 7 oz.) crabmeat, drained
  and flaked
¾ cup chili sauce

Blend sour cream and cream cheese until smooth. Stir in chopped vegetables, horseradish, lemon juice and oil. Spread about 2 tablespoons cream mixture over each crepe, then top each with 1 tablespoon crab and 1 tablespoon chili sauce. Roll up. Cover and chill until serving time. YIELD: 12 servings.

Caviar and Egg Appetizers

You can substitute 3 tablespoons finely chopped pimiento-stuffed green olives or 1 or 2 tablespoons anchovy paste for the caviar, if you wish.

12 (6½ to 7-inch) Crepes, halved
6 hard-cooked eggs, chopped
⅓ cup mayonnaise or salad dressing
2 tablespoons finely chopped onion
1 tablespoon vinegar or lemon juice
½ teaspoon prepared mustard
½ teaspoon salt
¼ teaspoon sugar
¼ teaspoon pepper or Dash hot
   pepper sauce
3 tablespoons well-drained caviar

In bowl combine eggs, mayonnaise, onion, vinegar, mustard, salt, sugar and pepper. Blend in caviar. Spread about 1 tablespoon mixture over each crepe half. Roll up. Cover and chill until serving time. YIELD: 24 appetizers.

Herbed Cheese Crepes

These savory little half-crepes make excellent appetizers or snacks.

8 Crepes (any size), halved
1 cup shredded Muenster or Monterey
   Jack cheese
¼ cup mayonnaise or salad dressing
1 teaspoon prepared mustard
½ teaspoon basil or oregano
¼ teaspoon onion salt

Combine cheese, mayonnaise, mustard and seasonings. Spread about ½ tablespoon over each crepe half. Fold each half circle in thirds to form cone or cornucopia. Arrange cones on greased baking sheet and bake in preheated 400°F. oven about 8 to 10 minutes. Serve hot. YIELD: 16 appetizers.

Swiss Crepe Appetizers

These hot little nibbles are perfect for holiday parties.

About 4 dozen (5½ to 6-inch) Crepes
2 tablespoons butter
¼ cup flour
½ teaspoon salt
¼ teaspoon paprika
1 cup milk
1 cup diced process Swiss cheese
1 egg, beaten
Egg wash*
2 cups corn flake crumbs

In saucepan melt butter. Add flour, salt and paprika and cook and stir over medium heat until bubbly. Add milk and cook and stir until smooth and thickened. Add cheese; stir just until melted. Add a small amount of hot mixture to egg, stirring constantly. Return to hot mixture; cook and stir until heated. Cover with plastic wrap and chill. For each appetizer spoon 1½ teaspoons cheese mixture in center of each crepe. Fold sides over filling and fasten with a wooden pick. Dip in egg wash and coat with crumbs. Fry in deep fat at 350°F., just until heated and browned, about 1 minute. Drain on absorbent paper. Serve hot. YIELD: About 4 dozen appetizers.

*EGG WASH: Combine 2 eggs and ¼ cup milk; beat. Repeat if needed.

Crepe Noodles

Fresher tasting than canned soup noodles, cooks faster than dry noodles. Your family will think you made them from rolled dough.

Crepes
Consomme, chicken broth or other favorite
   soup

Cut crepes into thin strips, about ¼-inch wide. Heat soup to boiling; add crepe strips. Reduce heat and simmer 5 minutes. YIELD: One 5½ to 6-inch crepe, cut up, makes enough noodles for 1 cup soup.

Tuna Pate Pinwheels

A tasty but very easy appetizer that you can prepare in advance to wait in the refrigerator.

10 (6½ to 7-inch) Crepes
1 package (3 oz.) cream cheese, softened
1 tablespoon chopped onion
1 tablespoon lemon juice
½ teaspoon curry powder
½ teaspoon salt
¼ teaspoon pepper
½ cup dairy sour cream
1 can (6½ or 7 oz.) tuna, drained and flaked

In mixing bowl beat cream cheese, onion, lemon juice, curry, salt and pepper until smooth. Blend in sour cream, then tuna. Spread about 3 tablespoons filling over each crepe. Roll up tightly. Cover and chill thoroughly. Cut each crepe crosswise into 1-inch pieces. Put out wooden picks to serve pinwheels.   YIELD: About 60 appetizers.

Chutney Cheese Stack
See photo page 14.

A wonderful make-ahead appetizer. Spread savory filling on crepes, then stack. Serve wedges with cocktails or along with soup for a first course.

6 (6½ to 7-inch) Crepes or 8 (5½ to
**   6-inch) Crepes**
1 package (8 oz.) cream cheese, softened
1 package (3 oz.) cream cheese, softened
½ cup chopped chutney
1 medium apple, cored and finely chopped
¼ cup finely chopped green pepper
**   or celery**
½ teaspoon grated lemon or lime peel
1 tablespoon lemon or lime juice

In mixing bowl combine cheese, chutney, apple, green pepper, lemon peel and juice and beat until well mixed. Arrange crepes in single layer on work surface and divide cheese mixture among crepes. Carefully spread cheese to edge of each crepe. Stack crepes on serving plate. Cover with plastic wrap and chill several hours. To serve, garnish with lemon slice. Cut with very sharp knife into 16 wedges.   YIELD: 16 appetizer portions.

Salmon Crepes with Caper Sauce

Arrange these little crepes on a pretty platter, with a bowl of Caper Sauce in the middle, for dipping.

24 (5½ to 6-inch) Crepes
1 can (16 oz.) salmon
2 tablespoons butter
2 tablespoons flour
½ cup milk
½ cup liquid from salmon
2 tablespoons grated onion
1 tablespoon lemon juice
1 teaspoon paprika
½ teaspoon salt
¼ teaspoon pepper
1 cup seasoned whole grain rye
**   cracker crumbs**

Drain salmon, reserving ½ cup liquid; flake salmon and set aside. In saucepan melt butter. Blend in flour and cook and stir over medium heat until bubbly. Add milk and reserved salmon liquid and cook and stir until smooth and thickened. Stir in lemon juice, paprika, salt and pepper, then mix in salmon and cracker crumbs. Cut each crepe in half. Spread 1 tablespoon filling on each crepe half; roll up. Serve with Caper Sauce for dipping.   YIELD: 48 appetizers.

CAPER SAUCE: Combine 1 cup dairy sour cream, ¼ cup chopped capers, 1 tablespoon caper juice, 1 tablespoon grated onion, salt and pepper to taste.

Cheese Tricorn Appetizers

Savory stuffed crepes make nice hot nibblers to serve with drinks or as a first course. You can prepare tricorns ahead and refrigerate, just add 5 to 10 minutes to heating time.

24 (6½ to 7-inch) Crepes
⅓ cup butter
¼ cup flour
1 cup milk
3 egg yolks
1 cup shredded Swiss cheese
1 cup diced Muenster cheese
½ cup grated Parmesan cheese
1 cup chopped pimiento-stuffed green olives
1 tablespoon grated onion
½ teaspoon salt
¼ teaspoon pepper
¼ teaspoon hot pepper sauce

In medium saucepan melt butter. Add flour and cook and stir over medium heat until bubbly. Add milk and cook and stir until smooth and thickened. Beat egg yolks and add a small amount of hot sauce to yolks. Mix well, then return yolk mixture to saucepan. Stir in cheeses just until melted. Remove from heat and mix in olives, onion and seasonings. Cut each crepe in half and spoon 1 tablespoon filling into center of each crepe. Fold two sides over filling to form a triangle or "tricorn." Bake in preheated 475°F. oven 10 minutes.   YIELD: 48 appetizers.

Crepe Dippers

Leftover or less-than-perfect crepes can be deep-fried to use as scoops for your favorite dip. Just wrap and freeze crepes as they accumulate, then fry when you have enough.

Crepes
Oil
Cut crepes into eighths to form small wedges. In saucepan or skillet heat at least 1½ inches of oil to 375°F. Add crepe pieces, a few at a time, and cook just until lightly browned. Turn and cook until lightly browned on second side. Remove to several thicknesses of paper towels and drain.

Sassy Shrimp Dip

A tangy dip to enhance delicate Crepe Dippers.

1 cup dairy sour cream
1½ tablespoons chopped parsley or parsley flakes
1½ teaspoons instant minced onion
1 teaspoon lemon juice
½ teaspoon salt
⅛ teaspoon cayenne pepper
1 to 2 drops hot pepper sauce
1 can (4½ oz.) small shrimp, rinsed and drained

Combine all ingredients except shrimp. Beat until well blended. Gently stir in shrimp. Cover with plastic wrap; refrigerate until serving time to blend flavors. Serve with Crepe Dippers, at left.   YIELD: About 1⅓ cups.

Guacamole Dip

This dip has zip. Try it with Corn Meal Crepe Dippers.

2 ripe avocados, peeled, pitted and mashed
⅓ cup finely chopped onion
1 tablespoon lemon juice
1 tablespoon mayonnaise
½ teaspoon chili powder
½ teaspoon garlic salt
1 medium tomato, peeled and finely chopped

Combine all ingredients except tomato; beat until well blended. Gently stir in tomato. Cover to blend flavors. Serve with Crepe Dippers, at left.   YIELD: About 3 to 3½ cups.

Dilly Dip

A light-flavored dip with a fresh taste.

1 cup dairy sour cream
¼ cup chopped green onions and tops
1 teaspoon Worcestershire sauce
½ teaspoon dried dill weed
¼ teaspoon garlic salt
¼ teaspoon salt

Combine all ingredients; beat until well blended. Cover with plastic wrap; refrigerate until serving time to blend flavors. Serve with Crepe Dippers, at left.   YIELD: About 1 cup.

CHICKEN AND TURKEY CREPES

Crepes are the perfect choice for a main course at a ladies' luncheon, a shower, brunch or bridge party. But don't think the other half of the world does not like them too. Recipes follow for sophisticated, simple, hearty and savory crepes that appeal to men, and kids as well.

A stack of crepes kept on hand in your freezer means you can put together a fancy meal or a quick-fix supper almost any evening. Just mix up the sauce or filling while the crepes stand at room temperature to thaw.

The main dish crepe recipes that follow run the gamut from very simple—with as few as 5 ingredients, most of them convenience foods —to sauced creations that require several ingredients and some culinary skill.

Since crepes are fork food, remember to keep pieces of food for the filling just bite-sized. Not only are crepes easier to eat, but they will be easier to fill and roll. When you begin to put together crepes for main dishes you will be surprised at how many ordinary entrees become special when dressed in a crepe.

Chicken Crepes Paprika

This could become your favorite crepe recipe. The rich, rosy sauce is just as good with cubed cooked veal, beef, pork, or even tuna.

16 (5½ to 6-inch) Crepes
2 tablespoons butter
2 tablespoons paprika
2 tablespoons flour
1 cup chicken broth or 1 cup hot water and
   1 chicken bouillon cube, crushed
1 cup dairy sour cream
2 tablespoons butter
⅓ cup chopped onion
1 cup chopped fresh mushrooms
1 tablespoon lemon juice
1 teaspoon salt
2 cups cubed cooked chicken

In medium saucepan melt 2 tablespoons butter. Add paprika and flour and cook and stir over medium heat until bubbly. Stir in chicken broth and cook and stir until smooth and thickened. Stir in sour cream. Keep warm but do not boil. In skillet melt butter. Add onion and saute until tender but not brown. Stir in mushrooms and cook another 3 to 5 minutes. Add lemon juice, salt and chicken and mix. Spoon about 2 tablespoons chicken mixture down center of each crepe. Roll up. Grease 13 x 9 x 2-inch baking pan and pour about ½ cup sauce from saucepan in. Arrange crepes in pan, then pour remaining sauce over. Bake in preheated 350°F. oven 15 minutes or until heated through.   YIELD: 8 servings.

The Queen's Own Crepes
See photo at left.

A poultry dish of royal status for a special family or company meal. Cooks up quickly.

12 Crepes (any size)
¼ cup butter
1½ cups sliced fresh mushrooms
   (about ¼ lb.)
¼ cup chopped onion
⅛ teaspoon thyme
2 cups diced cooked chicken
¼ cup snipped parsley
1 can (10¾ oz.) condensed cream of
   chicken soup
¼ teaspoon salt
Dash pepper
¼ cup light cream or half and half
2 tablespoons dry white wine

In skillet melt butter. Add mushrooms, onion and thyme and cook and stir over medium heat 2 to 3 minutes. Stir in chicken, parsley, ¾ cup of the soup, salt and pepper. Bring to boil, then reduce heat and simmer, stirring occasionally, until heated through.

Meanwhile, in saucepan combine remaining soup, cream and wine. Cook and stir over medium heat until hot and bubbly. Keep warm while rolling crepes. Spoon about ¼ cup chicken mixture down center of each crepe. Roll up. Top each crepe with about 1 tablespoon sauce.   YIELD: 4 to 6 servings.

Beautiful Broccoli Crepes

6 (5½ to 6-inch) Crepes
2 tablespoons butter
3 green onions, chopped
3 tablespoons flour
1 cup milk
½ teaspoon salt
2 cups diced cooked chicken
3 tablespoons sherry
1 lb. fresh broccoli
2 teaspoons lemon juice
½ teaspoon salt
Pimiento strips

In saucepan melt butter. Add onions and saute a minute or two. Blend in flour and cook and stir over medium heat until bubbly. Add milk and salt and cook and stir until thickened. Stir in chicken and sherry; keep hot. Cook broccoli in boiling salted water until tender. Drain; cut into individual stalks and sprinkle with lemon juice and salt. Roll 1 stalk broccoli in each crepe and arrange on warm serving plate. Spoon chicken sauce over. Garnish with pimiento strips.   YIELD: 6 servings.

Chicken a la King Crepes

12 Crepes (any size)
2 envelopes (⅞ oz. each) chicken gravy mix
1½ cups milk
½ cup sherry
2 egg yolks
½ cup whipping cream
2 cups diced cooked chicken
½ cup shredded Swiss cheese
2 tablespoons chopped pimiento
1 teaspoon chopped chives
¼ cup shredded Swiss cheese

In saucepan blend gravy mix with milk. Cook and stir over medium-high heat until thickened. Stir in sherry. Beat egg yolks and cream until blended, then stir into gravy. In mixing bowl combine chicken, ½ cup cheese, pimiento and chives. Stir in half the gravy mixture. Spoon about 2 tablespoons chicken mixture down center of each crepe. Roll up or fold. Arrange in greased 13 x 9 x 2-inch baking pan. Spoon remaining gravy mixture over crepes and sprinkle with ¼ cup cheese. Bake in preheated 350°F. oven 30 minutes.   YIELD: 4 to 6 servings.

22

Chicken-Celery Crepes

A great carry-along to a church or covered-dish supper. Cover pan and then insulate with a thick wrapping of newspapers to keep crepes hot.

12 (6½ to 7-inch) Crepes
¼ cup butter
1 cup finely chopped celery
¼ cup finely chopped onion
2 cups chopped cooked chicken or turkey
1 teaspoon seasoned salt
¼ teaspoon seasoned pepper
1 can (10½ oz.) condensed cream of celery soup
1 can (4 oz.) sliced mushrooms and liquid
¼ cup dry white wine
¼ cup shredded Cheddar cheese

In skillet or saucepan melt butter. Add celery an onion and saute until onion is tender but not brown. Stir in chicken and seasonings. In small bowl stir together soup, mushrooms and liquid and wine. Reserve ½ cup soup mixture for topping, stir remaining into chicken mixture. Spoon about ⅓ cup chicken mixture down center of each crepe. Roll up or fold and arrange in greased 9 x 13 x 2-inch baking pan. Spoon remaining soup mixture over and sprinkle with cheese. Bake in preheated 350° F. oven 25 minutes.   YIELD: 6 servings.

Chicken Crepes Taxco

The rich and creamy filling has just a light touch of Mexican seasonings. You could add a little more chili powder and chiles, if you wish.

12 (6½ to 7-inch) Crepes
2 cups cubed cooked chicken or turkey
2 cups dairy sour cream
1 cup shredded Cheddar or Monterey Jack cheese, divided
1 cup sliced green onions and tops
½ cup sliced ripe olives
2 to 3 tablespoons chopped green chiles
½ teaspoon chili powder
½ teaspoon ground cumin
½ teaspoon salt
1 can (8 oz.) tomato sauce with herbs

Combine chicken, sour cream, ½ cup of the cheese, onions, olives, chiles and seasonings. Spoon about ⅓ cup down center of each crepe. Roll up or fold and arrange in greased 9 x 13 x 2-inch baking dish. Pour tomato sauce over top and sprinkle with remaining cheese. Bake in preheated 350°F. oven 25 minutes. YIELD: 6 servings.

Chicken Tarragon Crepes

Tastes like the specialty of a French chef, but you don't have to tell that the sauce starts with a can of soup.

12 (6½ to 7-inch) Crepes
1 can (10¾ oz.) cream of chicken soup
⅓ cup milk
⅓ cup chopped celery
2 tablespoons lemon juice
1 teaspoon crushed tarragon leaves
2 cups cubed cooked chicken
¼ cup slivered almonds
2 tablespoons butter, melted

In mixing bowl blend soup, milk, celery, lemon juice and tarragon. Stir in chicken. Spoon about ¼ cup down center of each crepe. Roll up. Arrange crepes in greased 13 x 9 x 2-inch pan. Toss almonds with melted butter and scatter over top of crepes. Bake in preheated 375°F. oven about 30 minutes. YIELD: 6 servings.

Crepes a la Reine

Just a whiff of thyme adds an extra touch to this chicken-mushroom-wine sauce blend.

12 Crepes (any size)
¼ cup butter
¼ lb. fresh mushrooms, chopped
1 cup chopped celery
¼ cup chopped onion
⅛ teaspoon crushed thyme
1 can (10¾ oz.) condensed cream of chicken soup
1½ cups chopped cooked chicken
¼ teaspoon salt
Dash pepper
¼ cup light cream or half and half
2 tablespoons sauterne

In skillet melt butter. Add mushrooms, celery, onion and thyme and saute until tender. Stir in ¼ cup of the soup, chicken, salt and pepper. Heat through. Spoon about 3 tablespoons filling down center of each crepe. Roll up or fold, arrange on heatproof serving platter and keep warm in 300°F. oven. In saucepan combine remaining soup, cream and wine and heat until blended and bubbly. Spoon over crepes and serve at once. YIELD: 6 servings.

Crepes Mexicali

Not for the timid—a spicy crepe. Try them in Corn Meal Crepes.

12 Crepes (any size)
2 tablespoons butter
½ cup chopped onion
1 clove garlic, minced
2 cups chopped cooked chicken
1 can (8 oz.) tomato sauce
1½ to 2 tablespoons diced hot green chiles (about 1 chile pepper)
½ teaspoon salt
½ teaspoon basil, crushed
1 to 1½ cups shredded Cheddar, Longhorn, Colby or Monterey Jack cheese
Dairy sour cream

In saucepan or skillet melt butter. Add onion and garlic and saute until tender but not brown. Stir in chicken, tomato sauce, chiles, salt and basil. Bring to a boil, then reduce heat, cover and simmer 10 minutes. Spoon about ¼ cup chicken mixture down center of each crepe. Roll up. Arrange in greased 13 x 9 x 2-inch baking pan or dish. Sprinkle with cheese. Bake in preheated 350°F. oven 20 to 25 minutes or until cheese is melted and bubbly. Serve with dollops of sour cream. YIELD: 4 to 6 servings.

Creamy Chili Chicken Crepes

The smooth sauce has just enough chiles to please a tender palate. Add more chiles if you prefer a really hot mixture. Try Corn Meal Crepes here.

12 (6½ to 7-inch) Crepes
1 can (10½ oz.) golden mushroom soup
½ cup dairy sour cream
2 tablespoons chopped green chiles
1 tablespoon lemon juice
1 tablespoon instant minced onion
½ teaspoon salt
½ teaspoon cumin
2 cups diced cooked chicken
1 cup shredded Monterey Jack cheese

In mixing bowl combine soup, sour cream, chiles, lemon juice, onion, salt and cumin. Stir in chicken. Spoon about ¼ cup mixture down center of each crepe. Roll up or fold. Arrange crepes in greased 13 x 9 x 2-inch baking pan. Sprinkle with cheese. Bake in preheated 350° F. oven 30 minutes. YIELD: 4 to 6 servings.

Chicken Crepes Caribbean

12 (6½ to 7-inch) Crepes
2 whole chicken breasts
1½ cups water
½ teaspoon salt
2 tablespoons minced onion
1 tablespoon chopped parsley
3 tablespoons butter
3 tablespoons flour
⅓ cup pineapple juice
1 medium banana, sliced
1 cup seedless green grapes, halved
1 tablespoon lemon juice

Put chicken breasts in large heavy saucepan or skillet. Add water, salt, onion and parsley. Cover and simmer about 20 to 30 minutes or until chicken is done. Remove breasts from skillet. Skin, bone and cube chicken. Strain broth from skillet and measure 1 cup. In saucepan melt butter. Add flour and cook and stir over medium heat until bubbly. Add reserved 1 cup broth and pineapple juice and cook and stir until smooth and thickened. Taste and add additional salt, if necessary. Stir in chicken, banana, grapes and lemon juice and heat through. Spoon about ¼ cup down center of each crepe. Roll up. Spoon any remaining sauce over crepes to serve. Serve at once. YIELD: 6 servings.

Tasty Turkey Crepes

12 (6½ to 7-inch) Crepes
¼ cup butter
¼ cup chopped onion
¼ cup flour
1 teaspoon salt
½ teaspoon curry powder
2 cups milk
2 cups finely chopped cooked turkey
1 cup chopped nuts
1 egg, beaten
¼ cup shredded Cheddar cheese

In saucepan melt butter. Add onion and saute until tender but not brown. Blend in flour, salt and curry powder and cook and stir until bubbly. Add milk and cook and stir until thickened. Pour 1½ cups of the sauce into a mixing bowl. Add turkey and nuts to sauce in bowl and mix. Spoon about ¼ cup turkey mixture down center of each crepe. Roll up or fold. Arrange in greased 13 x 9 x 2-inch baking pan. Stir beaten

egg and cheese into sauce remaining in pan and heat until cheese melts. Spoon over crepes. Broil about 4 inches from heat until top is glazed. YIELD: 6 servings.

Chicken and Asparagus Crepes with Sherry Sauce

12 Crepes (any size)
¼ cup butter
¼ cup flour
½ teaspoon salt
½ teaspoon pepper
1¾ cups milk
1 can (5 oz.) boned chicken, chopped
1 jar (2½ oz.) sliced mushrooms, drained
¾ cup shredded Cheddar cheese
3 tablespoons sherry
1 can (15 oz.) extra-long green asparagus spears, drained

In saucepan melt butter. Add flour, salt and pepper and cook and stir over medium heat until bubbly. Stir in milk and cook and stir until smooth and thickened. Add chicken, mushrooms, cheese and sherry and heat through. Place 2 to 3 asparagus spears on each crepe and spread with 2 to 3 tablespoons chicken sauce. Roll up and arrange in greased 13 x 9 x 2-inch baking pan. Spoon remaining chicken sauce over crepes. Bake in preheated 350°F. oven 15 minutes. YIELD: 6 servings.

Curried Turkey Crepes

A super-quick dish for those ever-present after-the-feast leftovers. The grapes add a delightful color, flavor and texture contrast to the turkey.

12 (6½ to 7-inch) Crepes
1 can (10¾ oz.) condensed cream of onion soup
¼ cup milk
1 teaspoon curry powder
2 cups chopped cooked turkey
1 cup halved seedless green grapes
Toasted flaked coconut

Combine soup, milk and curry powder in large saucepan. Stir in turkey and grapes. Cook and stir over medium heat until hot and bubbly. Spoon scant ⅓ cup mixture down center of each crepe. Roll up. Garnish with coconut. YIELD: 6 servings.

Chicken-Mandarin Orange Crepes

12 (6½ to 7-inch) Crepes
2 cups finely chopped cooked chicken or turkey
½ cup drained and halved mandarin orange segments
½ cup chopped, drained water chestnuts
½ cup thinly sliced celery
⅔ cup mayonnaise or salad dressing, divided
¾ teaspoon salt
⅔ cup dairy sour cream
3 tablespoons sherry
⅓ cup toasted slivered almonds

In mixing bowl combine chicken, oranges, water chestnuts, celery, ⅓ cup of the mayonnaise and salt. Spoon about ⅓ cup chicken mixture down center of each crepe. Roll up or fold. Arrange in greased 13 x 9 x 2-inch baking pan. Combine sour cream, ⅓ cup mayonnaise and sherry and spoon over crepes. Sprinkle with almonds. Bake in preheated 350°F. oven 30 minutes.   YIELD: 6 servings.

Crepes Tetrazzini

12 (6½ to 7-inch) Crepes
¼ cup butter
½ cup chopped onion
¼ cup flour
½ teaspoon salt
¼ teaspoon pepper
⅛ teaspoon nutmeg
1 cup milk
1 cup chicken broth or water
¼ cup dry sherry
2 cups chopped cooked turkey or chicken
1 can (4 oz.) sliced mushrooms, drained
1 cup shredded Cheddar cheese

In skillet melt butter. Add onion and saute onion until tender but not brown, about 3 minutes. Blend in flour and seasonings. Cook and stir over medium heat until bubbly. Add milk and broth and cook and stir until mixture boils and is smooth and thickened. Remove from heat; blend in sherry. Add turkey and mushrooms. Spoon about ⅓ cup mixture down center of each crepe. Roll up. Arrange in greased 13 x 9 x 2-inch baking pan; sprinkle with cheese. Bake in preheated 350°F. oven 25 to 30 minutes or until hot and bubbly. YIELD: 6 servings.

Sweet Sour Turkey Crepes

12 (6½ to 7-inch) Crepes
1 can (8 oz.) pineapple chunks
1 tablespoon each cornstarch, sugar, soy sauce
⅛ teaspoon each ground ginger, garlic powder
2 cups diced cooked turkey
½ cup each sliced celery and green pepper
2 tablespoons sliced green onion and tops

Drain pineapple, reserving liquid. Add water to liquid, if necessary, to make ¾ cup. In saucepan stir together cornstarch, sugar, soy sauce, ginger and garlic powder. Add pineapple liquid and blend. Cook and stir over medium-high heat until mixture comes to a boil and is smooth and thickened. Stir in turkey, celery, green pepper and green onion and heat to boiling. Spoon about ¼ cup down center of each crepe. Roll up or fold. Serve at once.   YIELD: 6 servings.

Turkey Mushroom Crepes Mornay

8 (6½ to 7-inch) Crepes
2 tablespoons butter
2 tablespoons flour
1 cup milk or light cream or half and half
1 tablespoon instant minced onion
½ teaspoon salt
¼ cup grated Parmesan cheese
2 tablespoons sherry
2 cups diced cooked turkey
½ lb. sliced fresh mushrooms or 1 can or jar (4 oz.) sliced mushrooms, drained
2 tablespoons butter, melted
2 tablespoons grated Parmesan cheese

In saucepan melt 2 tablespoons butter. Blend in flour and cook and stir over medium heat until bubbly. Add milk, onion and salt and cook and stir until smooth and thickened. Stir in Parmesan and sherry until blended, then turkey and mushrooms. Spread about ¼ cup mixture over each crepe and roll up or fold. Arrange crepes in greased 13 x 9 x 2-inch baking pan or shallow pan. Brush tops of crepes with melted butter and sprinkle with 2 tablespoons Parmesan cheese. Bake in preheated 375°F. oven about 10 minutes.   YIELD: 4 servings.

MEAT AND MAIN DISH CREPES

Ham Apricot Crepes

See photo at left.

Use a package of cooked ham, slices of canned ham, or select other ham-type sliced meats from the cold cut section: chopped ham, luxury loaf, luncheon meat, etc.

10 (6½ to 7-inch) Crepes
10 thin slices ham or 1 package (8 oz.)
   cooked ham slices
1 can (8¾ oz.) apricot halves
2 tablespoons cornstarch
2 tablespoons brown sugar
Dash salt
1 can (12 oz.) apricot nectar
2 tablespoons butter
1 tablespoon lemon juice
1 teaspoon rum

Roll ham slices in crepes. Arrange in greased 13 x 9 x 2-inch baking pan. Drain apricots, reserving syrup. Arrange apricots over crepes in baking dish and keep warm in 300°F. oven while preparing sauce. In saucepan blend cornstarch, brown sugar and salt. Stir in reserved apricot syrup and apricot nectar. Cook and stir over medium heat until mixture comes to a boil and is smooth and thickened. Stir in butter, lemon juice and rum. Pour sauce over crepes in pan. Increase oven temperature to 400°F. and bake crepes 10 to 15 minutes or until heated through.   YIELD: 5 servings.

Sweet and Sour Crepes Oriental

Great for leftover roast pork, especially when time is short. The recipe is quick and easy.

12 (6½ to 7-inch) Crepes
1 can (15¼ oz.) pineapple chunks
Water
2 tablespoons cooking oil
1½ cups cubed cooked pork
1 package (2.12 oz.) sweet and sour
   sauce mix
1 cup halved cherry tomatoes
½ cup cubed green pepper

Drain pineapple, reserving syrup. Add water to syrup to make 1 cup. Set aside. Heat oil in skillet. Add pork cubes and brown lightly on all sides. Combine reserved pineapple liquid and sauce mix; stir into pork. Heat to boiling; stir in reserved pineapple, tomatoes and green pepper. Reduce heat, cover and simmer 10 minutes, stirring occasionally. Spoon scant ⅓ cup mixture down center of each crepe. Roll up.   YIELD: 6 servings.

Brathaus Crepes

A quick and easy delight for a hearty lunch or supper. Rye Crepes and a stein of beer are recommended go-alongs.

12 (6½ to 7-inch) Crepes
1 can (8 oz.) sauerkraut, well-drained
⅓ cup mayonnaise or salad dressing
2 tablespoons chili sauce
1 teaspoon caraway seed
6 bratwurst, cut in ½-inch slices
¾ cup shredded Swiss cheese

Combine sauerkraut, mayonnaise, chili sauce and caraway. Stir in sausage slices. Spoon scant ⅓ cup mixture down center of each crepe. Roll up. Arrange in greased 13 x 9 x 2-inch baking pan. Sprinkle with cheese. Bake in preheated 350°F. oven 15 to 20 minutes.
YIELD: 6 servings.

Ham Asparagus Crepes with Mushroom Sauce

Here's the recipe to show off at a special luncheon or party.

8 Crepes (any size)
3 tablespoons butter
2 jars (2½ oz. each) sliced mushrooms, drained
3 tablespoons flour
1 cup water
2 teaspoons instant chicken bouillon
⅓ cup light cream or half and half
¼ cup shredded Cheddar cheese
1 tablespoon chopped chives
8 slices cooked ham
4 large slices Swiss cheese, halved
1 can (15 oz.) extra-long green asparagus spears, drained

In saucepan melt butter. Add mushrooms and cook briefly. Stir in flour and cook and stir over medium heat until bubbly. Add water and chicken bouillon and cook and stir until thickened. Blend in cream, cheese and chives and keep hot. Put a ham slice, a cheese slice and 2 to 3 asparagus spears on each crepe and roll up. Arrange in greased 13 x 9 x 2-inch baking pan. Spoon mushroom sauce over. Bake in preheated 350°F. oven 25 minutes. YIELD: 4 servings.

Ham and Apple Brunch Crepes

Sweet and spicy but with just a little spunk, these crepes are great for special breakfasts and suppers as well as brunch.

6 (6½ to 7-inch) Crepes
2 large apples, pared, cored and sliced thin
1 tablespoon lemon juice
2 tablespoons butter
2 tablespoons brown sugar
½ teaspoon cinnamon
⅛ teaspoon dry mustard
1½ cups diced ham
½ cup dairy sour cream or plain yogurt

Toss apple slices with lemon juice to prevent darkening. In large skillet melt butter, add apples and cook until beginning to get soft. Sprinkle with brown sugar, cinnamon and dry mustard, then stir in ham and heat through. Spoon about ⅓ cup down center of each crepe. Roll up. Top each serving with spoonful of sour cream or yogurt.   YIELD: 6 servings.

Ham and Cheese Crepes with Mushroom Madeira Sauce

12 Crepes (any size)
3 tablespoons butter
½ lb. fresh mushrooms, sliced
3 tablespoons flour
¾ cup chicken broth or ¾ cup boiling water and 1 chicken bouillon cube, crushed
¼ cup Madeira wine
1 tablespoon chopped chives
1 teaspoon prepared horseradish
¼ cup light cream or half and half
12 thin slices cooked ham
12 thin slices Swiss cheese

In saucepan melt butter. Add mushrooms and saute until tender, about 5 minutes. Sprinkle flour over mushrooms and stir in. Add broth, wine, chives and horseradish and cook and stir over medium heat until thickened. Stir in cream and keep hot. Arrange a slice each of ham and cheese on each crepe. Roll up and arrange in greased 13 x 9 x 2-inch baking pan. Pour sauce over. Bake in preheated 350°F. oven about 25 minutes or until heated through. YIELD: 4 to 6 servings.

Tropical Ham and Egg Crepes

12 (6½ to 7-inch) Crepes
1 can (13½ oz.) crushed pineapple
1 can (10¾ oz.) condensed cream of chicken soup
1 cup dairy sour cream
6 hard-cooked eggs, chopped
1 cup diced cooked ham
1 tablespoon chopped chives
¼ teaspoon dry mustard
¼ cup grated Parmesan cheese

Drain pineapple, reserving ¼ cup syrup. In mixing bowl combine ½ can of the soup with drained pineapple, sour cream, chopped eggs, ham, chives and mustard. In measuring cup combine remaining ½ can soup with the reserved ¼ cup pineapple syrup. Spoon about ⅓ cup ham and egg filling down center of each crepe. Roll up. Arrange crepes in greased 13 x 9 x 2-inch baking pan. Spoon soup/syrup blend over. Sprinkle with Parmesan cheese. Bake in preheated 350°F. oven about 25 minutes or until hot through.
YIELD: 6 servings.

Delicate Ham and Mushroom Crepes

Be sure to buy Sunday's ham extra-big, so you'll have enough left over to make these crepes for a special mid-week supper.

8 (6½ to 7-inch) Crepes
1 tablespoon butter
½ lb. fresh mushrooms, sliced or 1 can (4 oz.) mushrooms, drained
¼ cup sliced green onions
1 cup dairy sour cream
2 cups diced cooked ham

In skillet melt butter. Add mushrooms and saute until tender. Stir in onions and sour cream, then ham. Spread about ⅓ cup ham mixture over each crepe. Roll up or fold. Serve at once. YIELD: 4 servings.

Ham Crepes Gateau

Instead of rolling crepes around filling, these crepes stack up, with rich ham-cheese-mushroom mixture in between each layer.

12 Crepes (any size)
¼ cup butter
2 tablespoons flour
½ teaspoon salt
Dash pepper
1 cup milk
½ cup grated Parmesan cheese
2 cups finely chopped cooked ham
2 cans (4 oz. each) mushroom stems and pieces, drained
2 tablespoons butter, melted
2 tablespoons grated Parmesan cheese

In saucepan melt ¼ cup butter. Blend in flour, salt and pepper and cook and stir over medium-high heat until bubbly. Add milk and cook and stir until smooth and thickened. Stir in ½ cup cheese, ham and mushrooms. Arrange one crepe in middle of greased shallow pan and spread with about 2 to 3 tablespoons ham mixture. Top with another crepe and spread with ham mixture. Repeat layers, ending with a crepe on top. Drizzle the 2 tablespoons melted butter over top crepe and sprinkle with the 2 tablespoons Parmesan cheese. Bake in preheated 350°F. oven 20 minutes. Cut in wedges to serve. YIELD: 6 servings.

Ham Crepes Florentine

Leftover ham is dressed up elegantly here. Serve along with a tossed salad, bread and wine.

12 (6½ to 7-inch) Crepes
2 tablespoons butter
2 tablespoons finely chopped shallots or green onions
½ lb. fresh mushrooms, sliced
1½ cups chopped cooked ham
1 package (10 oz.) frozen chopped spinach, cooked and well-drained
1 package (8 oz.) cream cheese, softened
½ to ¾ teaspoon dry mustard
½ teaspoon salt
¼ teaspoon nutmeg
Dash pepper
1 cup shredded Gruyere cheese

In large skillet melt butter. Add shallots and saute until tender, about 1 to 2 minutes. Add mushrooms and cook an additional 3 minutes. Add ham, spinach, cream cheese and seasonings. Cook and stir until cheese is melted and mixture boils, about 3 to 5 minutes. Spoon about ⅓ cup mixture down center of each crepe. Roll up. Arrange in greased 13 x 9 x 2-inch baking pan. Sprinkle with Gruyère cheese. Broil 6 inches from heat, just until cheese is melted, about 1 minute. YIELD: 6 servings.

Ham and Cheese Crepes

Try this filling in the Rye-Caraway variation of the Basic Crepe recipe.

12 Crepes (any size)
2 cups finely chopped cooked ham
1 cup shredded Cheddar, Swiss or Colby cheese
½ cup mayonnaise or salad dressing
¼ cup sweet or dill pickle relish, drained
2 tablespoons bottled mustard sauce
1 to 2 tablespoons pickle juice
1 tablespoon instant minced onion

In mixing bowl combine ham, cheese, mayonnaise, relish, mustard sauce, pickle juice and onion. Spread about 3 tablespoons over each crepe. Roll up or fold. Serve cold as finger food, or arrange on greased baking sheet and heat in preheated 350°F. oven 15 to 20 minutes. YIELD: 6 servings.

Ham and Cherry Crepes

Canned cherry pie filling makes the simple sauce. Another time try apple or raisin pie filling to top the creamy ham crepes.

12 (6½ to 7-inch) Crepes
2 cups finely chopped or ground cooked ham
1 package (8 oz.) cream cheese, softened
¼ cup dairy sour cream
2 tablespoons lemon juice or pickle juice
2 tablespoons chopped chives
1 can (21 oz.) cherry pie filling
2 tablespoons lemon juice
½ teaspoon cinnamon

In mixing bowl blend ham, cream cheese, sour cream, lemon juice and chives. Spread about ¼ cup ham mixture over each crepe and roll up. Arrange crepes in greased 13 x 9 x 2-inch baking pan. Stir together pie filling, lemon juice and cinnamon and spoon over crepes. Bake in preheated 350°F. oven about 25 minutes. YIELD: 6 servings.

Peachy Pork Crepes

Try this filling in Corn Meal or Pamesan Crepes. Sweet-sour filling gets just a little tang from lemon peel and juice.

8 (6½ to 7-inch) Crepes
1 lb. lean boneless pork, cut in ½ inch cubes
1 can (1 lb.) sliced cling peaches
1 can (11 oz.) mandarin orange segments
2 teaspoons cornstarch
1 teaspoon grated lemon peel
2 tablespoons lemon juice
1 tablespoon soy sauce
½ cup sliced celery

In skillet brown pork cubes on all sides. Meanwhile, drain peaches and oranges reserving syrup. Measure 1 cup syrup and add all but 2 tablespoons of syrup to skillet. Blend the 2 tablespoons with cornstarch and set aside. Cover skillet and simmer 15 to 20 minutes. Uncover and stir in syrup-cornstarch blend. Cook and stir until smooth and thickened. Add peaches and oranges along with lemon peel and juice, soy sauce and celery slices. Cook until heated through. Spoon about ½ cup down center of each crepe. Roll up or fold and serve at once. YIELD: 4 servings.

Polynesian Pork Crepes

See photo at right.

A very easy and very attractive encore for leftover roast pork. Bottled sweet-sour sauce gives you a head start.

12 (6½ to 7-inch) Crepes
2 cups cubed cooked pork
1 jar (10 oz.) sweet sour sauce
1 can (5 oz.) water chestnuts, drained and sliced
1 can (8 oz.) pineapple chunks, drained
½ cup cubed green pepper

In saucepan combine pork, sauce, sliced chestnuts, drained pineapple chunks and green pepper. Heat to boiling. Spoon about ¼ cup down center of each crepe. Fold in quarters to match photo, or roll up. Spoon any remaining sauce over. Serve at once. YIELD: 6 servings.

Pepper Steak Crepes

Round steak takes on an exciting flavor in this exotic combination.

12 (6½ to 7-inch) Crepes
¼ cup butter
1 clove garlic, minced
½ teaspoon ground ginger
1 lb. lean round steak or flank steak cut in very thin diagonal slices
2 green peppers, cut in strips
½ cup chopped onion
1 can (10½ oz.) beef broth
¼ cup soy sauce
2 tablespoons cornstarch
2 tomatoes, cut in wedges and then halved

In large skillet melt butter with garlic and ginger. Add steak slices; cook over medium heat about 2 minutes on each side until browned. Remove meat with slotted spoon; set aside. Cook green pepper and onion in remaining butter until tender but not brown, about 3 minutes. Combine broth, soy sauce and cornstarch. Stir into green pepper and onion. Add reserved meat. Cook, stirring gently until thickened and bubbly, about 3 to 5 minutes. Gently stir in tomatoes. Cook an additional 5 minutes. Spoon about ⅓ cup mixture down center of each crepe. Roll up.
YIELD: 6 servings.

Italian Beef Crepes

Cannelloni is the Italian version of crepes. This delicious recipe uses leftover roast beef or pot roast.

12 (6½ to 7-inch) Crepes
1 tablespoon oil
⅓ cup chopped onion
½ teaspoon basil
1 teaspoon flour
½ teaspoon salt
1 can (8 oz.) tomatoes
1 can (15 oz.) tomato sauce with tomato bits
2 tablespoons oil
⅔ cup chopped onion
1 teaspoon mixed Italian herbs
4 cups ground or finely chopped cooked beef
1 teaspoon salt
3 tablespoons chopped parsley
8 oz. Monterey Jack or Mozzarella cheese, sliced thin

In saucepan heat 1 tablespoon oil. Add ⅓ cup onion and basil and saute until tender but not brown, about 5 minutes. Stir in flour and ½ teaspoon salt, then add tomatoes and tomato sauce. Cook and stir until mixture comes to a boil and is thickened. Keep warm. In skillet, heat 2 tablespoons oil. Add ⅔ cup onion and herbs and saute until tender but not brown. Stir in beef, 1 teaspoon salt and parsley. Add 1 cup tomato sauce and mix. Divide beef mixture into 12 portions and roll a crepe around each portion. Arrange filled crepes, seam side down, in greased 13 x 9 x 2-inch baking pan. Pour remaining tomato sauce over. Arrange cheese slices on top of crepes. Bake in preheated 350°F. oven about 20 minutes. If desired, broil a minute or two to brown top.   YIELD: 6 servings.

Blue Burger Crepes

8 (6½ to 7-inch) Crepes
1 lb. lean ground beef
½ to 1 cup dairy sour cream
2 to 3 ounces blue cheese, crumbled
1 tablespoon instant minced onion

In skillet brown beef. Spoon off excess fat. Stir in sour cream, cheese and onion until blended. Spoon about ¼ cup beef mixture down center of each crepe. Roll up or fold. Serve at once or arrange crepes in greased shallow pan and heat in preheated 350°F. oven 20 minutes.   YIELD: 4 servings.

Creamy Beef and Tomato Crepes

See photo at right.

Use any lean, tender beef—such as tenderloin tips, round or good quality chuck steak. Try these crepes for a late evening supper, or a very special brunch.

8 (6½ to 7-inch) Crepes
2 tablespoons butter
1 lb. lean boneless beef, cut in ½-inch chunks
1 medium onion, sliced
¾ cup water
1 beef bouillon cube, crushed
1 cup dairy sour cream
1 cup halved cherry tomatoes

In skillet melt butter. Add beef and cook and stir over medium-high heat until browned. Push beef to one side of skillet, add onion and cook, separating into rings. Add water and bouillon cube. Cover and simmer 5 minutes, then uncover and simmer 5 more minutes. Blend in sour cream, then cherry tomatoes and heat through. Spoon about ¼ cup beef mixture down center of each crepe. Roll up. Spoon any remaining sauce over. Serve at once.
YIELD: 4 servings.

Chili Beef Crepes

This easy ground beef filling is mildly flavored. Hot chili fans will want to add more chili powder and more pepper.

12 (5½ to 6-inch) Crepes
1 lb. lean ground beef
¼ cup chopped onion
¼ cup chopped green pepper or celery
1 can (11 oz.) condensed tomato bisque soup
½ cup sliced pitted ripe olives
1 teaspoon lemon juice
½ teaspoon chili powder
½ teaspoon seasoned salt
1 cup shredded Monterey Jack or Cheddar cheese

In skillet cook beef, onion and green pepper until meat is browned. Spoon off any excess fat. Stir in soup, olives, lemon juice and seasonings and simmer about 5 minutes. Spoon about ¼ cup down center of each crepe and roll up or fold. Arrange in greased 13 x 9 x 2-inch baking pan. Sprinkle cheese over top. Bake in preheated 350°F. oven 15 minutes or broil about 5 inches from heat for 3 minutes or until cheese melts.   YIELD: 6 servings.

CREAMY BEEF AND
TOMATO CREPES ▶

Brandied Beef Crepes

These crepes are for VIPs—very important parties. And the filling is really quite easy to prepare.

12 (5½ to 6-inch) Crepes
2 tablespoons butter
1 lb. beef tenderloin, cut in ½ inch chunks
1 tablespoon butter
½ pound fresh mushrooms, sliced
¼ cup sliced green onions and tops
2 to 4 tablespoons brandy
1 carton (8 oz.) plain yogurt
½ teaspoon salt
Dash pepper

In skillet melt 2 tablespoons butter. Add beef and cook and stir over medium-high heat until browned. Push meat to one side of skillet, add the tablespoon of butter, mushrooms and onions and cook about 2 minutes. Lift meat, mushrooms and onions from skillet to bowl and set aside. Pour brandy into skillet and simmer about a minute, stirring crusted bits of meat from bottom of pan. Blend in yogurt, then return meat/mushroom mixture to pan and heat through. Spoon about 3 tablespoons meat mixture down center of each crepe. Roll up. Serve at once or arrange crepes in greased shallow pan and bake in preheated 350°F. oven about 15 minutes.   YIELD: 6 servings.

Almost Instant Stroganoff Crepes

A couple of canned items give you a real head start on this special entree.

12 (6½ to 7-inch) Crepes
1 lb. lean boneless beef, cut in ½ inch cubes
1 tablespoon butter
¼ cup water
1 can (10¾ oz.) condensed cream of onion soup
1 can (4 oz.) mushrooms and liquid
1 tablespoon instant minced onion
½ to 1 cup dairy sour cream
1 tablespoon chopped parsley

In skillet brown beef in butter. Add water; cover and simmer 10 to 15 minutes. Stir in soup, mushrooms and liquid, onion, sour cream and parsley and heat and stir until smooth. Spoon about ¼ cup down center of each crepe. Roll up. Arrange in greased 13 x 9 x 2-inch baking pan. Spoon any remaining sauce over. Bake in preheated 350°F. oven about 25 minutes.   YIELD: 6 servings.

34

Steaks in Crepes

You could brown steaks at the table, in a chafing dish, then assemble with a flair before your guests.

8 (6½ to 7-inch) Crepes
1 tablespoon butter
2 tablespoons chopped green onion
1½ tablespoons cornstarch
¾ cup water
⅓ cup white wine
2 beef bouillon cubes, crushed
1 teaspoon brandy
1 lb. beef top round, cut ¼-inch thick
Salt and pepper
3 tablespoons butter

In saucepan melt 1 tablespoon butter. Add green onion and saute briefly. Blend in cornstarch, then stir in water, wine and bouillon cubes. Cook and stir over medium heat until mixture comes to a boil and is thickened. Stir in brandy. Keep hot. Sprinkle beef with salt and pepper and pound very thin. Cut in 8 portions. In skillet heat butter. Add steak pieces and brown quickly on both sides. Put each piece of meat on a crepe and roll up. Serve immediately with wine sauce or arrange filled crepes in greased individual bakers and heat in preheated 300°F. oven 5 minutes. Top with wine sauce to serve.   YIELD: 4 servings.

Crepes South of the Border

A real family-pleaser, especially in Corn Meal Crepes. It is a dressy way to serve an inexpensive main dish.

12 (6½ to 7-inch) Crepes
1 lb. ground beef
¼ cup chopped onion
1 can (15 oz.) refried beans
1 can (8 oz.) tomato sauce, divided
¼ cup chopped green chiles
1 cup shredded Monterey Jack cheese

In large skillet brown beef with onion; drain. Stir in beans, ½ cup of the tomato sauce and chiles. Spoon ⅓ cup mixture down center of each crepe. Roll up. Arrange in greased 13 x 9 x 2-inch baking pan. Spread with remaining tomato sauce. Sprinkle with cheese. Bake in preheated 350°F. oven 20 minutes.
YIELD: 6 servings.

Poulet Jambon Crepes

An excellent way to use up those odds and ends of Easter leftovers. Colorful too.

12 (6½ to 7-inch) Crepes
2 tablespoons butter
2 tablespoons flour
½ teaspoon tarragon
¼ teaspoon salt
⅛ teaspoon pepper
¾ cup chicken broth
½ cup dry white wine
1 cup chopped cooked chicken
1 cup chopped cooked ham
2 hard-cooked eggs, chopped
¼ cup chopped green onions and tops
¾ cup shredded Swiss cheese

In large saucepan melt butter. Blend in flour and seasonings. Cook and stir over medium heat until smooth and bubbly. Add broth; cook and stir until smooth and thickened. Stir in wine. Add chicken, ham, eggs and onions. Spoon scant ⅓ cup mixture down center of each crepe. Roll up. Arrange in greased 13 x 9 x 2-inch baking pan. Sprinkle with cheese. Bake in preheated 350°F. oven 25 to 30 minutes.   YIELD: 6 servings.

Quick Gourmet Chicken Liver Crepes

12 (6½ to 7-inch) Crepes
¼ cup butter
1 lb. chicken livers, halved
½ cup chopped onion
1 can (10¾ oz.) condensed cream of celery soup
1 can (4 oz.) sliced mushrooms, drained
¼ cup dry red wine
½ teaspoon salt
⅛ teaspoon tarragon
Dash pepper
Dairy sour cream
Parsley, optional

Cook chicken livers in butter over medium heat, stirring to cook both sides until tender, about 5 minutes. Add onion; cook, stirring occasionally, an additional 3 minutes. Stir soup, mushrooms, wine and seasonings into chicken liver mixture. Cook and stir until hot and bubbly, about 5 minutes. Spoon about ⅓ cup mixture down center of each crepe. Roll up. Garnish with dollops of sour cream and parsley, if desired.   YIELD: 6 servings.

Crepes Ardennaises

A delightfully seasoned combination from France.

12 (6½ to 7-inch) Crepes
¼ cup butter
¼ lb. fresh mushrooms, sliced
1 clove garlic, minced
2 tablespoons flour
¼ teaspoon salt
⅛ teaspoon pepper
⅛ teaspoon nutmeg
Dash thyme
1 cup chicken broth
½ cup light cream or half and half
2 cups chopped cooked ham
¼ cup chopped green onions with tops
¾ cup shredded Gruyere cheese

In skillet melt butter. Add mushrooms and garlic and saute over medium heat about 5 minutes; remove with slotted spoon and set aside. Blend flour and seasonings with remaining butter. Cook and stir until bubbly. Add broth and cream and cook and stir until smooth and thickened. Stir in ham, onions and reserved mushrooms. Spoon scant ⅓ cup mixture down center of each crepe. Roll up. Arrange in greased 13 x 9 x 2-inch baking pan. Sprinkle with cheese. Bake in preheated 350°F. oven 25 to 30 minutes.   YIELD: 6 servings.

Cheese Chicken Crepe Quiches

For breakfast, brunch, lunch or dinner, these are sure to please.

12 (5½ to 6-inch) Crepes
½ cup finely chopped cooked chicken
½ cup shredded Cheddar cheese
4 eggs
1 can (10¾ oz.) condensed cream of mushroom soup
1 tablespoon instant minced onion
¼ teaspoon poultry seasoning

Line greased 3-inch muffin cups with crepes, being careful to avoid puncturing crepes. Place about 2 teaspoons chicken and 2 teaspoons cheese in each crepe-lined cup. Beat together eggs, soup, onion and poultry seasoning; pour about 2½ tablespoons egg mixture into each cup over cheese. Bake in preheated 375°F. oven 35 minutes or until knife inserted near center comes out clean. Let stand 5 minutes before serving.   YIELD: 6 servings.   NOTE: Refrigerate any leftovers.

FISH AND SEAFOOD CREPES

Perhaps it's the special touch that the French have with seafood that makes almost any fish or shellfish mixture seem right at home in a crepe. The delicate flavor and texture of fish are a perfect complement to lacy, tender crepes. Too, the fragrant and unusual sauces that go so well with crepes are perfect with fish. Almost every famous creperie stars a shrimp, sole, scallop or lobster specialty.

Now, with the recipes that follow, your own creperie can have several seafood attractions. A nice thing about crepe fillings is that sauces and extenders, such as chopped hard-cooked eggs, can make a small amount of seafood go a long way, pleasing the palate and the pocketbook. And remember, too, that the flavorful liquid from canned or frozen fish, or the cooking liquid from poached fish, can add extra flavor to sauces.

Fish and shellfish require a gentle touch when it comes to cooking—use low, even temperatures and do not over cook. Proper cooking times and temperatures produce delicate, tender fish—too high or too long gives tough products.

Unusual crepe batters go well with seafood sauces. Fresh or dried herbs added to the batter are particularly nice with fish fillings. Tarragon, rosemary, thyme, dill, oregano or basil add a special touch. Of course, lemon or lime peel are always nice with fish.

Fruits of the Sea Crepes

6 (6½ to 7-inch) Crepes
2 tablespoons butter
¼ cup chopped onion
**1 can (10½ oz.) condensed cream of
   shrimp soup**
1 tablespoon lemon juice
½ cup cooked peas
1 can (about 7 oz.) tuna, drained and flaked
2 hard-cooked eggs, chopped
1 cup sliced fresh mushrooms
¼ cup milk or light cream or half and half

In saucepan melt 1 tablespoon butter. Add onion and saute until tender. Stir in ½ cup of the soup, lemon juice, peas, tuna and eggs. Heat, stirring occasionally. Spoon about ¼ cup mixture down center of each crepe and roll up. Arrange on heatproof platter and keep warm in 300°F. oven. Meanwhile, in another saucepan melt remaining 1 tablespoon butter. Add mushrooms and saute. Stir in remaining soup and milk. Heat, stirring occasionally. Serve over crepes.   YIELD: 3 servings.

Sole Crepes Marguery
See photo at left.

12 (6½ to 7-inch) Crepes
1 lb. frozen fillets of sole
¼ cup water
¼ cup white wine
½ teaspoon salt
¼ teaspoon pepper
**1 can (10½ oz.) condensed cream of
   shrimp soup**
¼ cup milk
2 tablespoons sherry
2 tablespoons lemon juice
1 teaspoon instant minced onion

Put sole in skillet, add water, wine, salt and pepper. Cover and simmer about 15 minutes or until fish flakes with a fork. Lift fish from skillet to bowl and break into small chunks. Simmer liquid in skillet until reduced to about ¼ cup. Stir in soup, milk, sherry, lemon juice and onion. Mix 1 cup soup mixture with fish. Spoon about 3 tablespoons down center of each crepe. Roll up or fold. Arrange in greased 13 x 9 x 2-inch baking pan. Pour remaining soup mixture over crepes. Bake in preheated 350°F. oven 30 minutes.   YIELD: 6 servings.

Savory Seashore Crepes

This rich entree is as colorful as it is flavorful. Truly a special occasion dish!

12 Crepes (any size)
2 tablespoons butter
½ cup chopped onion
½ clove garlic, minced
1 cup mayonnaise or salad dressing
½ lb. cleaned cooked shrimp
1 package (6 oz.) frozen crabmeat, thawed, drained and flaked or 1 can (6½ oz.) crabmeat, drained and flaked
¾ cup finely chopped celery
½ teaspoon salt
Dash pepper
2 tablespoons butter, melted
½ cup soft bread crumbs

In saucepan or skillet melt 2 tablespoons butter. Add onion and garlic and saute until tender but not brown, about 3 minutes. Remove from heat. Combine with mayonnaise, shrimp, crabmeat, celery, salt and pepper. Spoon about ¼ cup filling down center of each crepe. Roll up. Arrange in greased 13 x 9 x 2-inch baking pan. Brush with melted butter; sprinkle with bread crumbs. Bake in preheated 350°F. oven 25 to 30 minutes or until hot and bubbly. YIELD: 6 servings.

Creamy Italian Tuna Crepes

Not red and spicy, but creamy white and delicately seasoned with herbs.

8 (6½ to 7-inch) Crepes
2 tablespoons oil
½ cup chopped onion
¼ cup chopped green pepper
1 can (9 oz.) tuna, drained and flaked
1 can (5⅓ oz.) evaporated milk
1 cup shredded Mozzarella cheese
1 tablespoon chopped parsley
½ teaspoon salt
½ teaspoon oregano or basil

In skillet heat oil. Add onion and green pepper and saute about 5 minutes. Stir in tuna, milk, cheese, parsley, salt and oregano until cheese melts. Spread about ¼ cup filling over each crepe. Roll up. Arrange on greased baking sheet or in greased 13 x 9 x 2-inch baking pan and heat in preheated 350°F. oven 15 minutes. YIELD: 4 servings.

Curried Crab Crepes

Very elegant, perfect for a special supper, luncheon or brunch. Another time, use shrimp, lobster, even tuna or chicken in place of crab.

12 (5½ to 6-inch) Crepes
1 package (6 oz.) frozen crabmeat, thawed
Milk
2 tablespoons butter
¼ cup chopped onion
1 teaspoon curry powder
2 tablespoons flour
½ teaspoon salt
2 hard-cooked eggs, chopped
1 medium apple, cored and chopped
1 to 2 teaspoons lemon juice
2 tablespoons *each* raisins, chopped peanuts and flaked coconut

Drain crab, reserving liquid. Add milk to liquid to make 1 cup. In saucepan melt butter. Add onion and curry powder and cook 3 to 4 minutes over medium heat. Blend in flour and salt and cook and stir until bubbly. Add milk-crab liquid and cook and stir until mixture is smooth and thickened. Stir in crab, eggs, apple and lemon juice. Spoon about ¼ cup mixture down center of each crepe. Roll up. Serve at once, or arrange crepes in greased baking dish or on greased baking sheet and keep hot in 300°F. oven for about 15 minutes. Combine raisins, peanuts and coconut and pass to sprinkle over crepes. YIELD: 6 servings.

Clam Quiche Crepes

Pretty little cups of clam and cheese-flavored custard, these are nice for light lunches or suppers.

12 (5½ to 6-inch) Crepes
1 can (6½ oz.) clams
1 cup shredded Cheddar cheese
4 eggs
¾ cup light cream or half and half
2 tablespoons chopped chives
½ teaspoon seasoned salt

Line greased 3-inch muffin cups with crepes, being careful not to puncture crepes. Drain clams, reserving liquid. Divide clams and cheese among crepe cups. Beat eggs, reserved clam liquid, cream, chives and salt together and pour into crepe cups. Bake in preheated 350°F. oven about 30 minutes or until knife inserted near center comes out clean. YIELD: 6 servings.

Scallop Crepes

12 Crepes (any size)
3 tablespoons butter
2 lbs. scallops, cut in half
¼ lb. fresh mushrooms, sliced
1 green onion, thinly sliced
1 tablespoon chopped parsley
3 tablespoons flour
1 teaspoon salt
Dash pepper
1½ cups light cream or half and half
⅓ cup dry white wine or ¼ cup water

In skillet melt butter. Add scallops, mushrooms, onion and parsley. Cover and simmer until scallops are tender, stirring often. Mix flour, salt and pepper; sprinkle over scallops and mix well. Add cream and wine and cook and stir over medium heat until thickened. Spoon 2 tablespoons of mixture down center of each crepe. Roll up. Arrange in greased 13 x 9 x 2-inch baking pan. Pour remaining sauce over crepes. Broil 3 to 4 inches from heat about 3 minutes or until top is glazed. YIELD: 4 servings.

Tasty Tuna Stacks

12 (5½ to 6-inch) Crepes
1 can (6½ or 7 oz.) tuna, drained and flaked
3 hard-cooked eggs, chopped
½ cup chopped celery
½ cup shredded Cheddar cheese
½ cup chopped sweet pickles
½ cup chopped onion
½ cup mayonnaise or salad dressing
1 tablespoon prepared mustard
1 tablespoon lemon juice
12 tomato slices
Grated Parmesan cheese

In mixing bowl combine tuna, eggs, celery, Cheddar cheese, pickles and onion. Blend mayonnaise, mustard and lemon juice. Add to tuna mixture and toss to mix. Spread each of 3 crepes with about ⅓ cup tuna mixture. Stack spread crepes, then top with another crepe and 4 tomato slices. Sprinkle with Parmesan cheese. Repeat for remaining crepes. Place on baking sheet. Bake in preheated 350°F. oven 25 to 30 minutes or until hot and Cheddar cheese is melted. Cut into quarters to serve. YIELD: 6 servings.

Salmon A La King Crepes

12 (6½ to 7-inch) crepes
1 can (1 lb.) salmon
¼ cup butter
¼ cup chopped onion
¼ cup chopped green pepper
¼ cup chopped celery
¼ cup all-purpose flour
1 teaspoon salt
½ teaspoon pepper
1½ cups light cream or half and half
1 jar (2 oz.) pimiento, drained and chopped
1 tablespoon lemon juice

Drain salmon, reserving liquid. Add water to liquid, if necessary, to make 1 cup. Flake salmon and set aside. In saucepan melt butter. Add onion, green pepper and celery and saute until tender but not brown. Blend in flour, salt and pepper and cook and stir over medium heat until bubbly. Stir in cream and reserved salmon liquid and cook and stir until smooth and thickened. Stir in salmon, pimiento and lemon juice. Heat just to boiling. Spoon about ½ cup down center of each crepe. Roll up or fold. Serve at once or arrange in greased 9 x 13 x 2-inch baking pan and bake in preheated 350°F. oven 25 minutes. YIELD: 6 servings.

California Tuna Crepes

10 Crepes (any size)
1 can (6½ or 7 oz.) tuna, drained and flaked
1 cup shredded Monterey Jack cheese, divided
½ cup dairy sour cream
¼ cup chopped green pepper
¼ cup chopped celery
¼ cup chopped pitted ripe olives
¼ cup coarsely chopped water chestnuts
2 tablespoons lemon juice
1 tablespoon instant minced onion
½ to 1 teaspoon chili powder

In mixing bowl combine tuna, ½ cup of the cheese, sour cream, green pepper, celery, olives, chestnuts, lemon juice, onion and chili powder. Spoon about 2 tablespoons tuna mixture down center of each crepe. Roll up. Arrange in greased 13 x 9 x 2-inch baking pan. Sprinkle remaining cheese over top. Bake in preheated 350°F. oven about 15 minutes or until cheese melts. YIELD: 5 servings.

Creole Fish Crepes

8 (6½ to 7-inch) Crepes
1 lb. frozen fish fillets, thawed
2 tablespoons butter
⅓ cup chopped onion
⅓ cup chopped green pepper
⅓ cup chopped celery
1 teaspoon salt
1 teaspoon sugar
1 bay leaf, crushed
¼ teaspoon thyme
1 can (1 lb.) tomatoes, chopped

Put fish in skillet and add 1 cup water. Cover and simmer slowly about 15 minutes or until fish flakes with a fork. Drain and set aside. In saucepan melt butter. Add onion and saute until tender but not brown. Add green pepper, celery and seasonings, then stir in tomatoes. Simmer, uncovered, about 10 minutes or until thick. Break fish into chunks with a fork and stir gently into sauce mixture. Spoon about ⅓ cup down center of each crepe. Roll up or fold. Serve at once. Spoon any remaining sauce over crepes.   YIELD: 4 servings.

Crab Crepes with Shrimp Sauce
See photo at left.

Two seafoods combine in a subtly-flavored curry mixture.

12 (6½ to 7-inch) Crepes
1 package (6 oz.) frozen crabmeat, thawed, drained and flaked
⅓ cup thinly sliced celery
2 tablespoons thinly sliced green onion
⅓ cup mayonnaise or salad dressing
2 tablespoons diced pimiento
1¼ teaspoons curry powder
2 teaspoons lemon juice
1 can (10½ oz.) condensed cream of shrimp soup
½ cup milk or light cream or half and half

In mixing bowl combine crab, celery, mayonnaise, onion, pimiento, curry powder and 1 teaspoon lemon juice; mix carefully. Spread about 2 tablespoons filling over each crepe. Roll up. Arrange crepes on heat-proof platter or in greased 13 x 9 x 2-inch baking pan. Bake in preheated 350°F. oven 15 minutes. While crepes are heating prepare sauce. Combine soup, milk and remaining 1 teaspoon lemon juice; stir over low heat until hot. Spoon sauce over crepes to serve.   YIELD: 6 servings.

Crab Crepes Au Gratin

If you are out to impress someone with a crepe recipe, here is the one! Corn Meal, Whole Wheat or Parmesan Batters are a good choice.

6 (6½ to 7-inch) Crepes
1 package (6 oz.) frozen crabmeat, thawed
Milk
3 tablespoons butter
3 tablespoons flour
½ teaspoon salt
½ teaspoon paprika
Dash pepper
1 cup light cream or half and half
1 tablespoon Worcestershire sauce
1 cup shredded Cheddar cheese, divided
¼ cup fine dry bread crumbs

Drain crab, reserving liquid. Add milk to liquid to make ½ cup. In saucepan melt butter. Add flour and cook and stir over medium heat until bubbly. Add cream and crab liquid/milk along with Worcestershire sauce. Cook and stir until mixture is smooth and thickened. Stir in ½ cup of the cheese and the crab. Spoon about ⅓ cup mixture down center of each crepe. Fold or roll up. Arrange in greased 13 x 9 x 2-inch baking pan. Sprinkle with remaining cheese and bread crumbs. Bake in preheated 350°F. oven 15 to 20 minutes.   YIELD: 6 servings.

Shrimp and Mushroom Sauced Crepes

Serve these crepes from a chafing dish at tableside. For an extra fillip, pass Hollandaise sauce to spoon over.

12 Crepes (any size)
1 lb. cleaned raw shrimp, cut in 1-inch pieces
1 cup sliced fresh mushrooms
2 tablespoons finely chopped onion
6 tablespoons butter
2 tablespoons flour
½ teaspoon salt
1 cup light cream or half and half
2 tablespoons chopped parsley

Fold crepes in quarters and arrange in chafing dish or electric skillet. In saucepan or skillet cook shrimp, mushrooms and onion in butter about 4 to 5 minutes. Sprinkle flour and salt over mixture and blend in. Add cream and cook and stir until thickened. Spoon shrimp sauce over crepes in chafing dish and heat through. Sprinkle with parsley.   YIELD: 6 servings.

Easy Tuna Crepes Hollandaise

12 Crepes (any size)
2 envelopes (1⅛ oz. each) Hollandaise
   sauce mix
1⅓ cups water
2 egg yolks
½ cup whipping cream
¼ cup sherry
2 cans (7 oz. each) tuna, drained and flaked
2 cups diced cooked shrimp

In saucepan blend Hollandaise sauce mix with water and heat to boiling. Beat egg yolks and cream until blended, then stir into sauce. Blend in sherry. Combine half the sauce mixture with the tuna and spoon about 2 tablespoons tuna mixture down center of each crepe. Roll up and arrange in greased 13 x 9 x 2-inch baking pan. Spoon remaining sauce mixture over. Broil about 4 inches from heat for 3 to 4 minutes or just until sauce topping is glazed.   YIELD: 6 servings.

Salmon Crepes Pacifica

12 (6½ to 7-inch) Crepes
1 can (16 oz.) salmon
¼ cup butter
½ lb. chopped fresh mushrooms
¼ cup chopped green onion
6 tablespoons butter
5 tablespoons flour
2 cups milk
1 cup light cream or half and half or
   whipping cream
¾ teaspoon salt
Dash Cayenne pepper
1½ cups shredded Swiss cheese
¼ cup grated Parmesan cheese

Drain salmon, reserving ¼ cup liquid. Flake salmon. In saucepan or skillet melt ¼ cup butter. Add mushrooms and green onion and saute until mushrooms are tender. Stir in salmon and reserved liquid. In another saucepan melt the 6 tablespoons butter. Blend in flour and cook and stir over medium heat until bubbly. Add milk and cream and cook and stir until smooth and thickened. Stir in salt and pepper. Measure ¾ cup cream sauce and stir into salmon mixture. Divide salmon mixture among crepes. Roll up or fold crepes. Stir Swiss cheese into cream sauce and heat until cheese melts. Spoon about 1 cup sauce over

bottom of greased 13 x 9 x 2-inch baking pan. Arrange filled crepes in pan and spoon remaining sauce over. Sprinkle with Parmesan cheese. Bake in preheated 350°F. oven 30 minutes.   YIELD: 4 to 6 servings.

Tuna Cheese Crepes

Golden cheese sauce and crepes make everyday tuna become something extraordinary.

12 Crepes (any size)
1 can (7 or 9 oz.) tuna, drained and flaked
½ teaspoon salt
½ teaspoon grated lemon peel
1 tablespoon lemon juice
Dash garlic salt
¼ cup butter
¼ cup flour or biscuit mix
½ teaspoon salt
¼ teaspoon pepper
2 cups milk
2 cups shredded process American cheese
Paprika
¼ cup slivered almonds

In mixing bowl mix tuna, salt, lemon peel and juice and garlic salt. Spoon about 1 tablespoon down center of each crepe. Roll up or fold, arrange in greased 13 x 9 x 2-inch baking pan and bake in 325°F. oven while preparing sauce (about 10 to 15 minutes). In saucepan melt butter. Blend in flour, salt and pepper and cook and stir over medium heat until bubbly. Add milk and cook and stir until smooth and thickened. Stir in cheese until melted. Spoon sauce over hot tuna-filled crepes. Sprinkle with paprika and almonds. Broil 4 to 5 inches from heat about 3 to 5 minutes or just until lightly browned.   YIELD: 6 servings.

Hollandaise Sauce

1 cup butter
3 egg yolks
½ teaspoon salt
Dash Cayenne pepper
3 tablespoons lemon juice

In small saucepan melt butter over low heat. Combine egg yolks, salt, pepper and lemon juice in blender container and blend on medium speed. While blender is running, slowly pour melted butter in. Continue to blend just until all butter is incorporated and mixture thickens slightly, about 15 to 30 seconds. YIELD: about 1⅓ cups.

Rich Creamed Crab Crepes

Truly mouth-watering, but not for the calorie counter.

12 Crepes (any size)
¼ cup butter
¼ cup flour
1½ cups light cream or half and half
½ teaspoon curry powder
½ teaspoon Worcestershire sauce
¼ teaspoon onion salt
Dash hot pepper sauce
1 package (6 oz.) frozen crabmeat or 1 can (7½ oz.) crabmeat, drained and flaked
Hollandaise Sauce (see page 42)
¼ cup white wine

In saucepan melt butter. Add flour and cook and stir over medium heat until bubbly. Add cream, curry powder, Worcestershire, onion salt and hot pepper sauce and cook and stir until smooth and thickened. Pour out ½ cup sauce and set aside. Stir crab into sauce in pan and heat through. Spoon about ¼ cup crab mixture down center of each crepe. Roll up or fold and arrange in greased 13 x 9 x 2-inch baking pan. Bake in preheated 300°F. oven 10 minutes. Meanwhile stir reserved sauce into Hollandaise Sauce along with wine and spoon over crepes to serve. YIELD: 6 servings.

Crab Crepes Gateau

Looking for a main dish to really impress someone? This is it!

12 (6½ to 7-inch) Crepes
¼ cup butter
¼ cup flour
½ teaspoon salt
Dash pepper
2¼ cups milk
¾ cup shredded Swiss cheese
1 package (6 oz.) frozen crabmeat or 1 can (7½ oz.) crabmeat, drained and sliced
2 tablespoons finely chopped green onion
Dash Worcestershire sauce
Dash hot pepper sauce
1 package (10 oz.) frozen chopped spinach
2 tablespoons minced onion
1 tablespoon butter
1 cup cottage cheese
Dash nutmeg

In saucepan melt ¼ cup butter. Add flour, salt and pepper and cook and stir over medium heat until bubbly. Add milk and cook and stir until smooth and thickened. Stir in Swiss cheese until melted. Measure 1 cup cheese sauce into small mixing bowl. Add crabmeat and green onion to cheese sauce in bowl along with Worcestershire and hot pepper sauce. Set aside. Cook spinach according to package directions; drain. In small skillet melt 1 tablespoon butter. Add onion and saute until tender. Stir in spinach, ¼ cup of cheese sauce, cottage cheese sauce and nutmeg. Arrange 1 crepe in greased shallow pan and spread with 1/6 of crab mixture. Top with another crepe and 1/6 of spinach mixture. Continue layering crepes and alternating crab and spinach filling. Spoon remaining cheese sauce over top. Bake in preheated 350°F. oven 30 minutes. Cut in wedges to serve. YIELD: 6 to 8 servings.

Shrimp Etouffe Crepes

The famous Louisiana seafood sauce goes beautifully into crepes. Be warned—this is a spicy mixture.

8 (6½ to 7-inch) Crepes
8 oz. frozen peeled cooked shrimp, thawed
½ teaspoon salt
⅛ teaspoon cayenne pepper
Dash black pepper
2 tablespoons oil
½ cup chopped onion
¼ cup chopped celery
¼ cup chopped green pepper
1 clove garlic, minced
¼ cup water
1 tablespoon Worcestershire sauce
Dash hot pepper sauce
1 tablespoon cornstarch
¼ cup water

Sprinkle shrimp with salt, cayenne and black pepper and set aside. In skillet heat oil. Add onion, celery, green pepper and garlic and saute 6 to 8 minutes, stirring frequently. Stir in ¼ cup water, Worcestershire sauce and hot pepper sauce, along with shrimp and simmer 10 minutes. Blend cornstarch and ¼ cup water and stir into shrimp mixture. Cook and stir until smooth and thickened. Spoon about ¼ cup shrimp mixture down center of each crepe. Roll up. Serve at once. YIELD: 4 servings.

Crepes Romaine

12 Crepes (any size)
3 tablespoons butter
3 tablespoons flour
1½ cups light cream or half and half
½ teaspoon salt
½ teaspoon dry mustard
Dash pepper
4 oz. boneless skinned smoked salmon or
    whitefish, cut in short strips
4 hard-cooked eggs, chopped
1 tablespoon drained capers
1 tablespoon chopped pimiento
1 teaspoon chopped chives

In saucepan melt butter. Add flour and cook and stir over medium heat until bubbly. Add light cream or half and half, salt, mustard and pepper and cook and stir until smooth and thickened. Stir in fish, eggs, capers, pimiento and chives and heat through. Spread each crepe with 2 tablespoons sauce. Roll up or fold and arrange in greased 13 x 9 x 2-inch baking pan. Spoon remaining sauce over. Bake in preheated 350°F. oven about 20 minutes or until heated through.   YIELD: 6 servings.

Crab Crepes Supreme

12 (6½ to 7-inch) Crepes
1 cup dairy sour cream
⅓ cup grated Parmesan cheese
¼ cup snipped parsley
1 tablespoon lemon juice
½ teaspoon salt
3 to 4 drops hot pepper sauce
2 packages (12 oz. each) frozen crabmeat,
    thawed, drained and flaked or 4 cans
    (6½ oz. each) crabmeat, drained and
    flaked
2 tablespoons butter, melted
½ cup soft bread crumbs
Lemon wedges
Parsley

In mixing bowl combine sour cream, cheese, parsley, lemon juice, salt and hot pepper sauce. Add crabmeat and toss. Spoon about ⅓ cup mixture down center of each crepe. Roll up. Place in greased 13 x 9 x 2-inch baking pan or dish. Brush with butter; sprinkle with bread crumbs. Bake in preheated 350°F. oven 20 to 25 minutes or until hot and bubbly. Garnish with lemon wedges and parsley, if desired.   YIELD: 6 servings.

Crab Crepes Mornay

12 (6½ to 7-inch) Crepes
1 package (6 oz.) frozen crabmeat, thawed
6 hard-cooked eggs, chopped
1 cup chopped celery
1 cup shredded Swiss cheese, divided
½ cup mayonnaise or salad dressing
½ teaspoon each dry mustard and salt
2 tablespoons butter
2 tablespoons flour
Milk
2 tablespoons white wine or lemon juice
¼ cup grated Parmesan cheese

Drain crabmeat, reserving liquid. Flake crabmeat and combine with eggs, celery, ½ cup of the cheese, mayonnaise, mustard and salt. Spread about ⅓ cup filling down center of each crepe. Roll up and arrange in greased 13 x 9 x 2-inch baking pan. In saucepan melt butter, blend in flour. Cook and stir over medium heat until bubbly. Add milk to reserved crab liquid to make 1¼ cups. Add to butter-flour mixture and cook and stir over medium heat until smooth and thickened. Remove from heat and stir in ½ cup Swiss cheese and wine until cheese melts. Pour over crepes. Sprinkle with Parmesan cheese. Bake in preheated 350° F. oven 30 minutes.   YIELD: 4 to 6 servings.

Crepes St. Jacques

12 (6½ to 7-inch) Crepes
¼ cup butter
½ clove garlic, minced
1 lb. scallops, cut into bite-sized pieces
½ lb. fresh mushrooms, sliced
¼ cup chopped green onions with tops
¼ cup all-purpose flour
½ teaspoon salt
1½ cups light cream or half and half
½ cup dry white wine
2 tablespoons snipped parsley
½ cup shredded Swiss cheese

In saucepan melt butter with garlic. Add scallops, mushrooms and onions. Cook over medium heat 5 minutes. Remove and set aside. Stir flour and salt into remaining butter. Add cream and cook and stir until smooth and thickened. Stir in scallop mixture, wine and parsley. Spoon about ⅓ cup mixture on each crepe. Roll up. Arrange in greased 13 x 9 x 2-inch baking pan. Sprinkle with cheese. Broil 6 inches from heat until cheese melts.   YIELD: 6 servings.

BLINTZES

Blintzes are the Jewish version of the crepe, but instead of rolling the crepe around the filling, blintzes capture savory fillings in a pocket shape. The distinctive fold for blintzes is shown in the step by step photos on page 00.

Blintz filling always goes on the browned side of the crepe, leaving the unbrowned side out. But, since blintzes get a quick trip through a buttered skillet, they become beautifully golden brown on that side too.

Traditional blintz fillings have a cottage cheese-sour cream base. Traditional blintzes may be served with a topping of sour cream, apple sauce or fruit. Canned pie filling makes a less-than-traditional, but very tasty, topper for many blintzes.

Once you've perfected the pocket idea of crepes you'll be ready to tuck in fillings other than cheese. Try chopped fresh or drained canned or frozen fruit, creamed meats or fish, sandwich spreads, even sliced hard-cooked eggs.

CHEESE BLINTZES page 47

Figure 1

Folding Blintzes

Blintz Fold holds traditional cheese filling inside crepes and is also nice for fruit fillings. Spoon filling in center of each crepe.

Fold one side over filling, Fig. 1, then bring other side over filling, Fig. 2. Bring one open end to center, Fig. 3, making fold at edge of filling.

Bring other open end in to center, Fig. 4, forming a neat little square pocket. If you should happen to have a few tablespoons of batter left, brush or dab on seams of blintz to help seal filling in while blintz is browning.

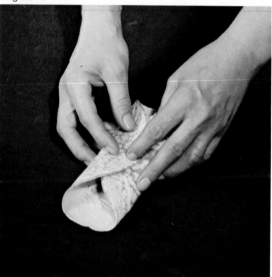

Figure 2 ▲   ▼ Figure 3

Figure 4

Cream Cheese Blintzes with Pineapple Sauce

A very simple filling and sauce.

16 (6½ to 7-inch) Crepes
1 package (8 oz.) cream cheese, softened
2 tablespoons light cream or half and half
2 tablespoons butter
1 can (6 oz.) frozen pineapple juice concentrate
2 cups sugar
½ cup butter
¼ cup water

Beat cream cheese and cream until fluffy. Dollop about 1 tablespoon in center of browned side of each crepe. Fold, following directions on page 00. In large skillet melt 2 tablespoons butter. Add blintzes, seam side down and brown lightly. Turn and brown other side. Meanwhile in saucepan combine pineapple juice concentrate, sugar, butter and water. Heat to boiling and boil 5 minutes, stirring occasionally. Spoon pineapple syrup over hot blintzes to serve.   YIELD: 6 servings.

Cheese Blintzes

See photo page 45.

Try fruit preserves to top these blintzes.

12 (6½ to 7-inch) Crepes
1 cup small curd cottage cheese
1 package (3 oz.) cream cheese, softened
¼ cup sugar
1 teaspoon vanilla extract
½ teaspoon grated orange or lemon peel
2 tablespoons butter
Dairy sour cream

In small mixing bowl combine cottage and cream cheese with sugar, vanilla and peel. Mix well. Spoon about 2 tablespoons cheese mixture into center of browned side of each crepe. Fold blintzes following directions on page 46. Cover and chill until serving time, if desired. In skillet or chafing dish melt butter. Add blintzes, seam side down, and cook until browned. Turn and cook on other side until golden brown. Serve hot, topped with sour cream.   YIELD: 6 servings.

All-American Apple Blintzes

Chopped nuts plus cubed Cheddar cheese in the filling make these a favorite dessert.

1 can (20 oz.) apple pie filling
1 cup cubed Cheddar cheese
½ cup chopped nuts
½ teaspoon cinnamon
12 (6½ to 7-inch) Crepes
3 tablespoons butter

In mixing bowl stir together pie filling, cheese, nuts and cinnamon. Spoon about 2 tablespoons into center of browned side of each crepe. Fold blintzes following directions on page 00. In large skillet melt butter. Add blintzes, seam side down and brown lightly. Turn and brown other side. Serve hot.
YIELD: 12 blintzes.

California Cottage Cheese Blintzes

Golden raisins add a special touch to this cheese filling.

8 (6½ to 7-inch) Crepes
1 cup small curd cottage cheese
1 package (3 oz.) cream cheese, softened
2 eggs
2 tablespoons sugar
½ teaspoon vanilla extract
⅓ cup golden seedless raisins
Dash salt
2 tablespoons butter
Dairy sour cream
Strawberry or raspberry preserves

In small mixing bowl beat together cheeses, eggs, sugar and vanilla. Stir in raisins and salt. Spoon about 2 tablespoons cheese mixture in center of browned side of each crepe. Fold blintzes following directions on page 00. In large skillet melt butter. Add blintzes, seam side down and brown lightly. Turn and brown other side. Serve hot, topped with sour cream and preserves.   YIELD: 8 servings.

VEGETABLE CREPES

Asparagus, Bacon and Egg Crepes

See photo at left.

A sunny special for any brunch. You could use broccoli or French-style green beans in place of asparagus.

8 (6½ to 7-inch) Crepes
2 tablespoons butter
2 tablespoons flour
1 cup milk
1 tablespoon instant minced onion
½ teaspoon salt
½ teaspoon dry mustard
4 to 6 slices bacon, crisp-cooked, drained and crumbled
6 hard-cooked eggs, chopped (reserve 1 egg yolk for garnish)
1 lb. asparagus, cooked and drained

In saucepan melt butter. Add flour and cook and stir over medium heat until bubbly. Add milk, onion, salt and dry mustard and cook and stir until smooth and thickened. Stir in bacon and eggs and keep hot. Divide asparagus spears among crepes, letting tips stick out at either end of crepes. Spoon sauce over asparagus on crepes. Roll up. Sieve reserved egg yolk and use to garnish crepes. Serve at once.
YIELD: 4 servings.

Somehow a vegetable becomes unique and extra-special when wrapped in a crepe. Many a light but satisfying main dish can be made from vegetables, richly sauced with cheese, cream and other ingredients. But a crepe full of cheesed carrots can be a surprise accompaniment to a slice of roast beef, a steak or chop, giving dinner plates a whole new lease on life.

One of the simplest and most delicious recipes in this book starts with frozen chopped spinach and adds just hard-cooked eggs, sour cream and onion soup mix. And you can make vegetable crepes even easier than that. Just prepare some of the new vegetables that come with their own sauce mix, then roll up in crepes. Voila—a vegetable occasion! And that old favorite casserole combination of mushroom soup, green beans and french fried onion rings takes on a whole new look when wrapped up in Parmesan or corn meal crepes. Or mix equal but small amounts of mayonnaise and sour cream to toss with cooked frozen mixed vegetables or slices of sauteed summer squash. Asparagus seems designed to be wrapped in a crepe.

Swiss Carrot Crepes

Cook carrots only until they are crisp-tender so the filling will be slightly crunchy. These crepes make a surprisingly good main dish, as well as a delicious side dish.

8 (6½ to 7-inch) Crepes
2 tablespoons water
2 tablespoons butter
1 vegetable bouillon cube
4 cups shredded carrots
½ teaspoon seasoned salt
1 cup shredded Swiss cheese

In large saucepan heat water, butter and bouillon cube until cube dissolves. Add carrots. Cover and cook over medium-high heat about 5 minutes or just until carrots are crisp tender. Pour off any excess liquid (save for soups or stews). Stir in cheese until melted. Spoon about ¼ cup down center of each crepe. Roll up. Serve at once.   YIELD: 4 to 8 servings.

Garden Vegetable Crepes

In August or September use zucchini, in mid-winter substitute frozen cut green beans, cauliflower or chopped broccoli. These crepes are nice as a side dish or an entree.

12 (5½ to 6-inch) Crepes
2 tablespoons butter
½ cup chopped onion
1 clove garlic, minced
2 tablespoons flour
1 can (8 oz.) tomato sauce with herbs
½ cup chicken broth or ½ cup boiling water
   and 1 chicken bouillon cube, crushed
2 cups sliced zucchini or 1 package (10 oz.)
   frozen cut green beans, cauliflower or
   chopped broccoli
⅔ cup chopped green pepper
1 tablespoon chopped parsley
1 teaspoon salt
1 teaspoon basil

In skillet or large saucepan melt butter. Add onion and garlic and saute until tender but not brown. Add flour and blend. Stir in tomato sauce and broth and cook and stir until mixture comes to a boil and is thickened. Add zucchini, green pepper, parsley, salt and basil. Cover and simmer 5 minutes. Uncover and simmer 5 minutes longer. Spoon about 2 tablespoons filling down center of each crepe. Roll up and serve at once.   YIELD: 6 servings.

Magnificent Mushroom Crepes

12 Crepes (any size)
½ cup butter
3 lbs. fresh mushrooms, sliced
¼ cup finely chopped onion
2 tablespoons flour
1 cup light cream or half and half
2 tablespoons sherry
1 tablespoon lemon juice
½ teaspoon salt

In large skillet melt butter. Add mushrooms and onion and saute. Sprinkle flour over mushrooms and stir to blend. Gradually stir in cream, then add sherry, lemon juice and salt. Cook and stir until smooth and thickened. Spoon about ¼ cup down center of each crepe. Roll up. Serve at once or arrange crepes in greased 13 x 9 x 2-inch baking pan and heat in 350°F. oven about 15 minutes.
YIELD: 6 servings.

Pois Pot Pourri Crepes

12 (6½ to 7-inch) Crepes
3 tablespoons butter
½ cup chopped onion
3 tablespoons flour
1 teaspoon salt
1 cup milk
1 cup chicken broth
1 package (10 oz.) frozen peas*
1 package (10 oz.) frozen sliced carrots*
¼ teaspoon dried dill weed

In large saucepan over medium heat cook onion in butter until tender but not brown, about 3 minutes. Blend in flour and salt. Cook and stir until smooth and bubbly. Stir in milk and broth. Cook and stir until smooth and thickened. Add frozen peas, frozen carrots and dill weed, stirring to blend well. Cook and stir until bubbly. Cover; reduce heat. Simmer, stirring occasionally, 10 minutes or until vegetables are of desired degree of doneness. Spoon about ⅓ cup mixture down center of each crepe. Roll up.   YIELD: 6 servings.

*Vegetables can be separated before cooking by gently striking against counter edge.

Mushroom Bechamel Crepes

12 Crepes (any size)
¼ cup butter
1 lb. fresh mushrooms, sliced
1 cup diced onions
2 tablespoons flour
¼ teaspoon salt
⅛ teaspoon pepper
⅛ teaspoon nutmeg
Dash thyme
1 cup chicken broth
½ cup light cream or half and half

In skillet melt butter. Add mushrooms and onions and saute until tender but not brown, about 5 minutes. Remove with slotted spoon; set aside. Stir flour and seasonings into remaining butter. Cook and stir over medium heat until bubbly. Add broth and cream; cook and stir until smooth and thickened. Reserve ½ cup sauce. Stir mushroom mixture into remaining sauce. Spoon about ¼ cup mixture down center of each crepe. Roll up. Spoon 2 teaspoons reserved sauce over each crepe.
YIELD: 4 to 6 servings.

Garden Brunch Crepes

Use vegetables fresh from your garden for this pretty and flavorful hearty brunch dish.

12 (6½ to 7-inch) Crepes
2 tablespoons butter
½ cup chopped onion
½ cup diced green pepper
2 to 3 firm tomatoes, wedged*
½ teaspoon garlic salt
½ teaspoon basil
Dash pepper
12 eggs
¾ cup milk
1½ teaspoons seasoned salt
¼ teaspoon pepper
¼ cup butter

In small skillet cook onion and green pepper in 2 tablespoons butter over medium heat until tender but not brown, about 3 minutes. Stir in tomatoes, garlic salt, basil and dash pepper. Continue cooking 5 minutes. Keep warm while preparing eggs. Beat together with a fork or rotary beater eggs, milk, salt and ¼ teaspoon pepper. Heat ¼ cup butter in large skillet or large saucepan over medium heat until just hot enough to sizzle a drop of water. Pour in egg mixture. As mixture begins to set, gently draw a pancake turner completely across bottom and around sides of pan, forming large, soft curds. Continue until eggs are thickened throughout but still moist, avoiding constant stirring. Spoon about ⅓ cup scrambled eggs down center of each crepe. Roll up. Top each crepe with scant ¼ cup vegetable mixture. Serve immediately. YIELD: 6 servings. *Peel, if desired.

Cheesy Cauliflower Crepes

Tangy and terrific. You need not be a vegetarian to enjoy these.

12 (6½ to 7-inch) Crepes
1 medium head cauliflower
1 cup shredded Cheddar cheese
½ cup mayonnaise or salad dressing
1 tablespoon instant minced onion
2 teaspoons prepared mustard
1 teaspoon salt
2 tablespoons butter, melted
½ cup soft bread crumbs

Wash cauliflower. Break into flowerets. Cook in boiling salted water 15 minutes; drain well. Meanwhile, combine cheese, mayonnaise, onion, mustard and salt. Place about ¼ cup cauliflower mixture on each crepe. Spread with about 1 tablespoon cheese mixture. Roll up. Arrange in greased 13 x 9 x 2-inch baking pan. Brush with butter; sprinkle with bread crumbs. Bake in preheated 350°F. oven 15 minutes or until cheese is melted.
YIELD: 6 servings.

Broccoli Delight Crepes

The soup mixture becomes a no-fail mock Hollandaise for the broccoli—and it is so easy!

2 packages (10 oz. each) frozen chopped broccoli, cooked and well-drained
1 can (10½ oz.) condensed cream of onion soup
¼ cup mayonnaise or salad dressing
1 tablespoon lemon juice
2 tablespoons grated Parmesan cheese

In large saucepan combine broccoli, soup, mayonnaise and lemon juice. Cook and stir over medium heat until hot and bubbly, about 5 minutes. Spoon scant ⅓ cup mixture down center of each crepe. Roll up. Sprinkle each crepe with ½ teaspoon cheese.
YIELD: 6 servings.

Creamed Beans Amandine

12 Crepes (any size)
2 packages (10 oz. each) frozen French-style green beans, cooked and well-drained
1 can (10½ oz.) condensed cream of celery soup
2 tablespoons dry white wine
1 tablespoon lemon juice
1 tablespoon instant minced onion
3 tablespoons butter
¼ cup sliced blanched almonds

In large saucepan combine beans, soup, wine, lemon juice and onion. Cook and stir over medium heat until hot and bubbly, about 5 minutes. Meanwhile, in small skillet melt butter, add almonds and cook over medium heat until browned, about 5 minutes. Spoon about ¼ cup bean mixture down center of each crepe. Roll up. Top each crepe with 1 teaspoon almonds with butter.
YIELD: 6 servings.

Spicy Spinach Crepes

Easy to do party vegetable dish with a surprise seasoning!

12 (6½ to 7-inch) Crepes
2 packages (10 oz. each) frozen chopped spinach
2 tablespoons butter
½ lb. fresh mushrooms, sliced
1 package (8 oz.) cream cheese, softened
1 package (0.6 oz.) Italian salad dressing mix
2 tablespoons butter, melted
2 tablespoons grated Parmesan cheese

Cook spinach according to package directions; drain *well.* Meanwhile, saute mushrooms in 2 tablespoons butter 5 to 6 minutes; remove from heat. Add drained spinach, cream cheese and salad dressing mix; stir until cheese is melted. Spoon scant ⅓ cup filling down center of each crepe; roll up. Arrange in greased 13 x 9 x 2-inch baking pan or on baking sheet. Brush with melted butter. Sprinkle with Parmesan cheese. Broil 6 inches from heat until cheese browns, 1 to 2 minutes. YIELD: 6 servings.

VARIATION: Substitute 2 packages (10 oz. each) frozen chopped broccoli for spinach and ½ teaspoon seasoned salt for Italian salad dressing mix. Delete melted butter. Top crepes with tomato slices and Parmesan cheese before broiling.

Herbed Spinach and Cheese Crepes

The cheese filling and tomato sauce will remind you of Lasagne, only better. This recipe could become a family favorite.

12 Crepes (any size)
2 packages (10 oz. each) frozen chopped spinach, cooked and very well-drained
1 tablespoon butter, melted
¾ teaspoon salt
Dash pepper
1 cup small curd cottage cheese
3 eggs, beaten
⅓ cup light cream or half and half or milk
2 tablespoons grated Parmesan cheese
Dash nutmeg
1 tablespoon butter, melted
¼ cup grated Parmesan cheese
1 can (8 oz.) tomato sauce with herbs

In mixing bowl combine spinach, 1 tablespoon butter, salt and pepper. Stir in cottage cheese, eggs, cream, 2 tablespoons Parmesan and nutmeg. Divide spinach mixture among crepes. Roll up. Arrange in greased 13 x 9 x 2-inch baking pan. Brush with the 1 tablespoon melted butter and sprinkle with remaining Parmesan cheese. Bake in preheated 350°F. oven 30 minutes. Heat tomato sauce and pass to pour over crepes. YIELD: 6 servings.

Speedy Spinach Crepes

Keep some crepes and chopped spinach on hand in the freezer and this recipe can be your emergency "special." It only has 5 ingredients but tastes like you spent hours in the kitchen.

12 Crepes (any size)
1 package (10 oz.) frozen chopped spinach, cooked and well-drained
4 hard-cooked eggs, chopped
1½ cups dairy sour cream
½ envelope (about 2 tablespoons) onion soup mix

In mixing bowl combine spinach, eggs, sour cream and soup mix. Spoon about ¼ cup down center of each crepe. Roll up or fold. Arrange crepes in greased 13 x 9 x 2-inch baking pan or shallow pan and bake in preheated 350°F. oven about 25 to 30 minutes or until very hot. YIELD: 6 servings.

Polish Crepes with Sauerkraut Stuffing

18 Crepes (any size)
2 tablespoons butter
½ cup chopped onion
1 can (4 oz.) sliced mushrooms, drained
1 cup well-drained sauerkraut
1 teaspoon salt
¼ teaspoon pepper
1 hard-cooked egg, chopped
1 cup dairy sour cream
2 eggs
½ cup fine dry bread crumbs
¼ cup butter

Melt 2 tablespoons butter in skillet. Add onion; cook until light golden brown. Add mushrooms, sauerkraut, salt and pepper. Cook over medium-high heat until sauerkraut becomes a golden color. Remove from heat; stir in hard-cooked egg and ¼ cup of the sour cream. Spoon a rounded tablespoonful of sauerkraut mixture onto center of each crepe. Fold 2 opposite edges of crepe over filling, then fold 2 ends into the center. Beat eggs. Roll crepes in egg, then in bread crumbs and pan fry in remaining butter until golden brown, turning once. Serve with remaining sour cream.
YIELD: 6 servings.

Mediterranean Vegetable Crepes

Brightly-colored and richly-flavored, these crepes make an excellent main dish or side dish.

10 to 12 (6½ to 7-inch) Crepes
3 tablespoons oil
1 medium onion, chopped
1 clove garlic, minced
2 medium zucchini, cubed or sliced
½ medium green pepper, diced
1 stalk celery, chopped
1 small eggplant, peeled and diced
4 medium tomatoes, peeled and chopped or
   1 can (1 lb.) tomatoes, chopped
½ cup sliced pitted ripe olives (optional)
2 tablespoons chopped parsley
1½ teaspoons salt
1 teaspoon sugar
½ teaspoon pepper

In skillet heat oil. Add onion and garlic and saute until tender but not brown, about 5 minutes. Add vegetables; cover and simmer 20 minutes. Uncover and simmer about 5 minutes longer or until thick enough to spoon. Spoon about 1 cup vegetable mixture over bottom of greased 13 x 9 x 2-inch baking pan. Spoon about ½ cup vegetable mixture down center of each crepe. Roll up crepes and arrange on vegetables in baking pan. Spoon any remaining vegetable mixture over top. Bake in preheated 375°F. oven about 10 minutes or until heated through.   YIELD: 5 to 6 servings.

EGG AND CHEESE CREPES

Cheese Fondue Crepes

See photo at left.

A savory accompaniment or protein stretcher for a special meal. Prepare them ahead if you like.

12 (6½ to 7-inch) Crepes
1½ cups shredded Swiss cheese
1 package (8 oz.) cream cheese, cubed
3 tablespoons dry white wine
1 tablespoon Kirschwasser
3 tablespoons butter
½ teaspoon dry mustard
¼ teaspoon garlic powder
Cooking oil
1 egg, slightly beaten

Combine cheeses, wine, Kirschwasser, butter, mustard and garlic powder in heavy saucepan. Cook over low heat, stirring constantly until cheeses are melted. Remove from heat. Spoon about 2½ tablespoons cheese mixture onto center of each crepe. Fold 1 side up to cover filling; tuck ends in. Complete rolling with remaining side. Heat oil ½-inch deep in skillet to 375°F. Meanwhile, dip crepes into egg. Fry in oil, 1 minute on each side, turning carefully to avoid puncturing crepes. Serve with Mustard Sauce.   YIELD: 6 servings.

NOTE: Refrigerate any leftovers. To reheat: broil 6 inches from heat 1 to 2 minutes.

The gentle flavors and textures of egg and cheese fillings make them ideal for wrapping in crepes.

Egg salad mixtures, creamed eggs, sauced sliced eggs, even plain old scrambled eggs somehow seem to taste better in a crepe package. And, since eggs are always handy in the refrigerator, you've got the basis of many a crepe filling (as well as many a crepe) right at hand.

Cheeses, too, are perfect crepe partners. Just a simple sprinkling of cheese on a crepe is a fix-up worthy of attention. Or wrap a slice of cheese in a crepe and heat—as simple as a sandwich but call it Crepes Au Fromage and you've become a gourmet.

Start thinking of batter variations to team with egg and cheese fillings and you could go on forever—Parmesan, Herb, Corn Meal, Oatmeal, Whole Wheat, Lemon, and so on.

Mustard Sauce

Terrific on Cheese Fondue Crepes!
Quick and easy to prepare too.

2 tablespoons butter
1½ tablespoons flour
½ teaspoon dry mustard
¼ teaspoon salt
Dash nutmeg
½ cup milk
¼ cup chicken broth or water
1½ teaspoons prepared mustard

In saucepan melt butter. Stir in flour, dry mustard, salt and nutmeg. Cook and stir over medium-high heat until bubbly. Add remaining ingredients; cook and stir until mixture boils and is smooth and thickened.   YIELD: About ¾ cup.

Fiesta Favorites

See photo at right.

You may want to double this recipe. They'll go fast! Fiesta Favorites also make fantastic appetizers.

4 (6½ to 7-inch) Corn Meal Crepes
Cooking oil
½ to ¾ cup tomato sauce with onion
¾ to 1 cup shredded Monterey Jack,
   Longhorn or Colby cheese
1 package or can (6 to 7¾ oz.) frozen
   avocado dip, thawed or ¾ to 1 cup
   homemade guacamole

Cut each crepe into 8 wedges. Heat oil ¼-inch deep in skillet to 375°F. Fry crepe wedges until crisp and brown, turning once, about 30 seconds on each side. Drain on paper toweling. Rearrange crepe wedges into crepe shapes on baking sheet. Spread each crepe with 2 to 3 tablespoons tomato sauce and sprinkle with 3 to 4 tablespoons cheese. Broil 6 inches from heat until cheese is melted and bubbly. Dollop with avocado dip. Serve immediately.   YIELD: 4 servings.

Lorraine Crepe Quiches

Individual serving portions of a French classic. Easy but elegant.

12 (5½ to 6-inch) Crepes
6 slices bacon, cooked, drained and
   crumbled
½ cup shredded Swiss cheese
¼ cup finely chopped green onions and tops
4 eggs
1 cup whipping cream, light cream or
   half and half
½ teaspoon salt
Dash nutmeg, optional

Line greased 3-inch muffin cups with crepes, being careful to avoid puncturing crepes. Place about 1 tablespoon bacon, 2 teaspoons cheese and 1 teaspoon onion in each crepe-lined cup. Beat together eggs, cream and seasonings; pour about 2½ tablespoons egg mixture into each cup over onions. Bake in preheated 375°F. oven 30 minutes or until knife inserted near center comes out clean. Let stand 5 minutes before serving.   YIELD: 6 servings.   NOTE: Refrigerate any leftovers.

Easy Elegant Egg Cups

These pretty-as-a-picture individual egg servings will delight your brunch guests. Cook them to order by altering the baking time.

12 (5½ to 6-inch) Crepes
12 eggs, large size or smaller
¾ cup light cream or half and half
6 slices bacon, cooked, drained
   and crumbled
1 tablespoon grated Parmesan cheese

Line greased 2¾ or 3-inch muffin cups with crepes being careful to avoid puncturing crepes. Break an egg into each crepe-lined cup. Spoon 1 tablespoon cream over each egg. Sprinkle each with about 1 tablespoon bacon bits and ¼ teaspoon cheese. Bake in preheated 325°F. oven 15 to 25 minutes or until eggs are of desired degree of doneness.
YIELD: 6 servings.

VARIATIONS: *Chived Cheese*—Substitute 1 tablespoon chopped chives and ¾ cup sliced mushrooms, drained, for bacon bits and grated Parmesan cheese.

Mushroom Onion—Substitute 2 tablespoons finely chopped onion and 1 can (2 to 2½ oz.) sliced mushrooms, drained, for bacon bits and grated Parmesan cheese.

56

Curried Egg Salad Crepes

The curry flavor is very mild and peanuts add a pleasant crunch.

12 (6½ to 7-inch) Crepes
10 to 12 hard-cooked eggs, chopped
½ cup mayonnaise or salad dressing
½ cup chopped salted peanuts
⅓ cup dairy sour cream
¼ cup finely chopped celery
1 teaspoon curry powder
½ teaspoon salt
1 can (10¾ oz.) cream of chicken soup
¼ cup milk
2 tablespoons lemon juice
¼ cup chopped salted peanuts

In large mixing bowl combine eggs, mayonnaise, ½ cup peanuts, sour cream, celery, curry powder and salt. Spoon about ⅓ cup filling down center of each crepe. Roll up. Arrange in greased 13 x 9 x 2-inch baking pan. Blend soup, milk and lemon juice and pour over crepes. Sprinkle with the ¼ cup peanuts. Bake in preheated 350° F. oven 30 minutes.

YIELD: 4 to 6 servings.

Italian Cheese Crepes

Rich cheese filling, tangy tomato sauce and a double cheese topping make these crepes something extra special. You can put this dish together in advance, cover and refrigerate to reheat come dinner time. Add another 10 minutes to baking time if prepared in advance and chilled.

18 (6½ to 7-inch) Crepes
1 lb. Ricotta cheese
3 eggs
½ cup grated Parmesan cheese
½ cup well-drained, chopped, cooked spinach
1 teaspoon seasoned salt
Dash pepper
2 cans (8 oz. each) tomato sauce with herbs or onions
1 cup shredded Mozzarella cheese
¼ cup grated Parmesan cheese

In mixing bowl combine Ricotta, eggs, ½ cup Parmesan, spinach, seasoned salt and pepper and mix well. Spoon about 2 tablespoons down center of each crepe. Roll up and arrange in greased 13 x 9 x 2-inch baking pan or on greased jelly roll pan. Pour tomato sauce over crepes, then sprinkle with Mozzarella and ¼ cup Parmesan cheese. Bake in preheated 375°F. oven 15 to 20 minutes or until heated through.   YIELD: 6 servings.

Cheese and Bacon Crepes

Rich and hearty, these are a good choice for apres-ski or wintry brunches. Try using Parmesan Crepes here.

12 (6½ to 7-inch) Crepes
6 slices bacon, chopped
1 medium onion, chopped
2 cups shredded Cheddar cheese
½ teaspoon celery salt

In skillet cook bacon until crisp. Remove and drain, reserving 2 tablespoons drippings. In reserved drippings saute onion until tender but not brown. Remove from heat and stir in bacon, cheese and salt. Spread about 2 tablespoons cheese mixture over each crepe and roll up. Arrange in greased 13 x 9 x 2-inch baking pan and bake in preheated 350°F. oven 10 to 15 minutes.   YIELD: 6 servings.
NOTE: these crepes are nice halved for appetizer servings.

Oeufs Brouilles Au Jambon Crepes

Great for a special breakfast or brunch. Pretty, elegant and practical.

12 Crepes (any size)
2½ tablespoons butter
½ lb. cooked ham, diced (about 1½ cups)
8 eggs
⅓ cup milk
2 teaspoons chopped chives
½ teaspoon salt
Dash pepper
¾ cup shredded Swiss cheese

In large skillet or saucepan melt butter. Add ham and cook over medium heat until lightly browned, about 5 minutes. Mix eggs, milk and seasonings with a fork or rotary beater. Pour egg mixture over ham; cook over medium heat. As eggs begin to set, gently draw a pancake turner across bottom and around sides of pan, forming large, soft curds. Continue until eggs are thickened but still quite moist, avoiding constant stirring. Spoon about ¼ cup ham and egg mixture down center of each crepe. Roll up. Arrange in greased 13 x 9 x 2-inch baking pan. Sprinkle with cheese. Broil 6 inches from heat just until cheese melts. Serve immediately.   YIELD: 6 servings.

Breakfast Bounty Crepes

When making these crepes, keep in mind the fresher the eggs, the less they will spread. Your family or guests will be delighted to discover their breakfast eggs so smartly dressed.

12 (6½ to 7-inch) Crepes
12 *very fresh* eggs, large size or smaller
6 slices bacon, cooked, drained and crumbled
12 thin slices tomato
2 tablespoons grated Parmesan cheese
Dairy sour cream

Arrange crepes in single layer on greased baking sheet. Working directly on baking sheet carefully break an egg into the center of each crepe. Sprinkle each egg with about 1 tablespoon bacon. Gently lap sides of crepe over egg. Without pressing down, top each crepe with a tomato slice and sprinkle with ½ teaspoon cheese. Bake in preheated 325°F. oven 15 minutes or until eggs are of desired degree of doneness. To serve dollop with sour cream.   YIELD: 6 servings.

Cheese Strata Crepes

A great make-ahead brunch recipe with day-old bread! The egg mixture puffs the bread into a delightful mound of goodness.

12 (5½ to 6-inch) Crepes
2 slices day-old bread
Butter
¾ cup shredded Cheddar cheese
4 eggs
1 cup milk
2 teaspoons instant minced onion
1 teaspoon dry mustard
½ teaspoon salt
Dash pepper

Line greased 3-inch muffin cups with crepes, being careful to avoid puncturing crepes. Butter bread; cut into small cubes. Place 1 tablespoon bread cubes and 1 tablespoon cheese into each crepe-lined cup. Beat together eggs, milk and seasonings; pour about 2½ tablespoons egg mixture into each cup over bread and cheese. Cover with plastic wrap; refrigerate several hours or overnight. Bake in preheated 350°F. oven 60 minutes or until golden brown.   YIELD: 6 servings.

NOTE: Refrigerate any leftovers.

DESSERT CREPES

Crepe desserts are so versatile, so delicious and so easy that they can star at numerous parties or special occasions: After-theater crepes, after-the-game crepes, after-dinner crepes, after-bridge crepes, even after-school crepes.

Anything sweet and smooth can be wrapped in a crepe to become a sweet tooth tempter. Ice cream, surrounded by a crepe and topped by sundae sauce, fresh fruit, thawed frozen fruit or liqueur, becomes instant elegance.

Look to the Batter Section for the many different batters that can be the basis of desserts. Chocolate Crepes, used instead of Dessert Crepes, give you a whole new menu star with just a change in batter.

The Create Your Own Section that follows gives you plenty of dessert ideas. But, first give some of these recipes a try—they'll become your favorites!

Brandied Peach Crepes

See photo at left.

Plan on another 2 to 3 tablespoons of apricot brandy so you can flame these beautiful golden crepes.

12 Crepes (any size)
1 package (10 or 12 oz.) frozen sliced peaches, thawed
¼ cup sugar
1 tablespoon cornstarch
Dash salt
½ cup water
1 tablespoon butter
2 tablespoons apricot brandy

Drain peaches, reserving syrup. In saucepan combine sugar, cornstarch and salt. Add reserved peach syrup and water and blend. Cook and stir over medium heat until mixture boils and is smooth and thickened. Stir in butter, brandy and peaches. Heat through. Spoon about 1 cup mixture into chafing dish or heat-proof serving dish. Spoon about 1 tablespoon peach mixture down center of each crepe. Roll up or fold and put on top of sauce in chafing dish to serve. YIELD: 6 servings.

Pineapple Puffs

A simply luscious treat. Serve them any time of the day.

1 recipe Souffle Crepes Batter, uncooked
24 well-drained pineapple slices
Powdered sugar

Over medium heat, pour 2 tablespoons batter into seasoned crepe or omelet pan. Place 1 pineapple slice on batter; quickly pour an additional 2 tablespoons batter over pineapple slice. Cook both sides until browned, about 1 minute on each side. Dust with powdered sugar. Keep cooked crepes warm in 200°F. oven while completing cooking.
YIELD: 6 to 8 servings.

Citrus Meringue Crepes Gateau

So impressively pretty your guests will never guess how easy these meringue-capped stacks are to prepare. Serve them for a light and refreshing meal finale.

12 (5½ to 6-inch) Dessert Crepes
1 package (3 oz.) lemon-flavored pudding and pie filling mix
¾ cup sugar, divided
3 tablespoons water
1 tablespoon orange juice concentrate
2 eggs, separated
2 cups water
⅛ teaspoon cream of tartar

In saucepan combine pudding mix, ½ cup of the sugar, 3 tablespoons water and orange juice concentrate. Stir in egg yolks and 2 cups water. Cook and stir over medium heat until mixture comes to a full boil. Remove from heat. Cool 5 minutes, stirring occasionally. Meanwhile, beat egg whites and cream of tartar until soft peaks form. Add remaining sugar, 1 tablespoon at a time, beating constantly until sugar is dissolved* and whites are glossy and again stand in soft peaks. Spread scant ¼ cup pudding mixture on each of 6 crepes. Stack crepes on ovenproof platter or serving dish. Repeat for remaining 6 crepes to form a second stack. Spread ½ of the meringue on each crepe stack over hot filling, swirling over side of stack to bottom, completely and evenly covering all filling and crepes. Bake in preheated 425°F. oven 5 minutes or until tips are lightly browned. Cool at room temperature. Cut into wedges to serve.

YIELD: 8 to 12 servings.

*Rub just a bit of meringue between thumb and forefinger to feel if sugar has dissolved.

California Sunshine Crepes

You can make dessert an occasion with this sauce. And the recipe makes enough for a group.

24 Crepes (any size)
2 teaspoons grated orange peel
⅔ cup orange juice
½ cup sweet butter
2 tablespoons honey
¼ cup brandy
¼ cup orange-flavored liqueur
Powdered sugar

In chafing dish or crepe finishing pan simmer orange peel, juice, butter and honey for 2 to 3 minutes. Dip crepes in sauce and fold in quarters, setting each crepe aside on plate after it is dipped. When all crepes are dipped return them to pan. In small saucepan warm brandy and orange liqueur. Pour over crepes and ignite with long-handled match. Spoon sauce over crepes until flames die down. Sprinkle with powdered sugar to serve.
YIELD: 10 to 12 servings.

Cherry-Sauced Crepes

Cottage cheese inside, dark sweet cherries outside and goodness all around. This is a great family dessert.

12 Dessert or Vanilla Crepes (any size)
1 cup small curd cream-style cottage cheese
⅓ cup dairy sour cream
3 tablespoons sugar
1 can (17 oz.) pitted dark sweet cherries
2 tablespoons sugar
1 tablespoon cornstarch
1 tablespoon lemon juice

Combine cottage cheese, sour cream and 3 tablespoons sugar. Spoon 1 heaping tablespoon onto each crepe. Roll up and arrange in buttered 13 x 9 x 2-inch baking pan. Bake in preheated 325°F. oven 10 minutes. Drain cherries, reserving syrup. In saucepan stir together 2 tablespoons sugar and cornstarch; then stir in reserved cherry liquid and lemon juice. Cook and stir over medium-high heat until mixture comes to a boil and is smooth and thickened. Stir in cherries and heat through. Spoon over hot crepes to serve.
YIELD: 6 servings.

Peaches and Cream Crepes

A pretty dessert—good for unexpected company. Most ingredients are probably on hand.

16 (5½ to 6-inch) Dessert Crepes
1 can (29 oz.) sliced peaches
½ cup sugar
3 tablespoons cornstarch
⅛ teaspoon salt
1 tablespoon lemon juice
1 tablespoon butter
Cinnamon-sugar
Whipping cream, whipped

Drain peaches, reserving ½ cup syrup. Set aside. In saucepan combine sugar, cornstarch and salt; stir in reserved peach syrup. Cook and stir over medium-high heat until thickened, about 2 to 3 minutes. Stir in reserved peaches, lemon juice and butter. Continue cooking until hot and bubbly. Spoon about 2 tablespoons peach mixture in center of each crepe. Fold 1 side up over filling; tuck ends in. Complete rolling with remaining side. Sprinkle with cinnamon-sugar and dollop with whipped cream. YIELD: 6 to 8 servings.

NOTE: For cinnamon-sugar, combine 1½ teaspoons cinnamon with ¼ cup sugar.

Apple Crepe Tarts

Easier than pie, delicious and pretty. They will be gone in no time!

16 Dessert Crepes (any size)
¼ cup butter
5 cups peeled, cored and sliced tart apples (about 2 lbs.)
½ cup sugar
1 teaspoon cinnamon
½ cup shredded Cheddar cheese

In large skillet over medium heat cook apples with sugar and cinnamon in butter stirring occasionally until apples are tender and glazed, about 7 to 10 minutes. Spoon about ¼ cup mixture on half of each crepe; fold remaining half of crepe up over filling. Arrange on greased baking sheet. Sprinkle with cheese. Broil 6 inches from heat until cheese is melted, 1 to 2 minutes.   YIELD: 8 to 16 servings.

Crepes Ambrosia

A great dessert for weight watchers. For the non-calorie-conscious, substitute whipped cream for the sour cream.

12 to 16 Dessert Crepes (any size)
1 cup drained pineapple chunks
1 cup halved orange segments or drained mandarin orange segments*
1 cup banana slices*
½ cup flaked coconut
½ cup dairy sour cream
Dairy sour cream
Grated orange peel

Combine fruits, coconut and ½ cup sour cream. Spoon about ¼ cup mixture down center of each crepe; roll up. Garnish with dollops of sour cream and a sprinkling of orange peel.   YIELD: 6 to 8 servings.

*3 cups well-drained fruit may be substituted for pineapple, oranges and bananas. Try berries!

Viennese Crepes

See photo at right.

Cottage cheese, currants and grated lemon peel are the rich and flavorful filling for these crepes.

16 Crepes (any size)
¼ cup butter
¼ cup sugar
1 teaspoon vanilla extract
1 teaspoon grated lemon peel
½ teaspoon salt
1 egg
1 cup small curd cottage cheese
¾ cup currants
1 tablespoon flour
1½ cups milk
1 egg
¼ cup sugar
2 tablespoons toasted slivered almonds

Cream butter until light. Add the ¼ cup sugar, vanilla, peel and salt and mix. Beat in 1 egg, then stir in cottage cheese, currants and flour. Spread about 2 tablespoons cheese mixture over each crepe. Roll up. Arrange in greased 13 x 9 x 2-inch baking pan. In small mixing bowl beat milk, 1 egg and ¼ cup sugar. Pour over crepes. Bake in preheated 350°F. oven 30 minutes. Sprinkle with toasted almonds to serve.   YIELD: 8 servings.

Brandied Cherry-Cinnamon Sauce

A spicy fruit sauce delicious over lemon pudding or ice cream-filled crepes.

1 can (16 oz.) red tart pitted cherries
½ cup sugar
3 tablespoons cinnamon red hot candies (about 1½ oz.)
2 tablespoons cornstarch
2 tablespoons brandy (cherry-flavored, if desired)
1 tablespoon lemon juice

Drain cherries, reserving all but 2 tablespoons liquid. Set aside. In saucepan combine sugar, candies and cornstarch. Stir in reserved cherry liquid. Cook and stir over medium-high heat until mixture thickens and boils and candies are dissolved.* Remove from heat. Stir in reserved cherries, brandy and lemon juice. Chill before serving.

YIELD: About 2¼ cups.

*Stir vigorously to dissolve candies.

Almond Cream Crepes

Delightful in Almond Extract-Flavored Crepes.

12 to 16 Dessert Crepes (any size)
½ cup sugar
3 tablespoons cornstarch or ⅓ cup all-purpose flour
¼ teaspoon salt
3 cups milk
3 egg yolks
1 teaspoon almond extract
¾ teaspoon vanilla extract
½ cup chopped toasted almonds, divided
Powdered sugar

In a large saucepan combine sugar, cornstarch and salt. Combine milk and egg yolks. Stir a little of milk mixture into sugar mixture to make a smooth paste. Gradually stir in remaining milk mixture. Cook and stir over medium heat until mixture boils and is smooth and thickened. Boil and stir 1 additional minute. Remove from heat and blend in extracts. Stir in ¼ cup of the almonds. Cover with plastic wrap; chill. Just before serving spoon scant ¼ cup mixture down center of each crepe. Roll up. Sprinkle with powdered sugar and remaining almonds.

YIELD: 6 to 8 servings.

NOTE: Refrigerate any leftovers.

Double Strawberry Crepes

See photo at right.

Strawberry jam fills the crepes, a sauce from fresh or frozen berries goes over the top.

12 Crepes (any size)
¾ to 1 cup strawberry jam
1 pint fresh strawberries
½ cup sugar

Spread each crepe with about 1 tablespoon jam. Fold in quarters. Wash and hull berries. Garnish top of crepes with whole berries or put half the berries into blender container with sugar and blend until smooth. Slice remaining berries and add to blended mixture. Spoon sauce over crepes to serve.

YIELD: 6 servings.

NOTE: you can use 1 package (10 oz.) frozen sweetened berries in place of fresh berries and sugar.

Amande a l'Orange Crepes

An exciting meal finale! Another time serve the orange sauce over ice cream or pudding-filled crepes.

20 Dessert Crepes (any size)
¼ cup butter, melted
2 eggs, slightly beaten
2 tablespoons grated orange peel
⅓ cup orange juice
¼ cup sugar
2 teaspoons grated lemon peel
1½ tablespoons lemon juice
1¼ cups toasted slivered almonds
Powdered sugar

In saucepan combine butter, eggs, orange peel, orange juice, sugar, lemon peel and lemon juice; mix well. Cook and stir over medium heat until mixture thickens and boils, about 3 to 5 minutes. Spoon 1 tablespoon almonds down center of each crepe; top with 1 tablespoon hot orange sauce. Roll up. Dust with powdered sugar.

YIELD: 10 to 20 servings.

Brandy Alexander Crepes

Well worth the effort; these crepes are ideal prepare-aheads for entertaining. A light but luscious dessert to follow a hearty meal.

12 Chocolate or Cocoa Crepes (any size)
½ cup sugar, divided
1 envelope unflavored gelatin
½ cup water
2 eggs, separated
1 package (3 oz.) cream cheese, softened
3 tablespoons brandy
3 tablespoons Creme de Cacao
¼ teaspoon cream of tartar
1 cup whipping cream, divided
Chocolate curls, optional

In saucepan combine ¼ cup sugar and gelatin; stir in water. Cook and stir over low heat until gelatin is dissolved, about 3 minutes. Remove from heat. Beat egg yolks until thick and lemon-colored, about 5 minutes. Blend a little of hot gelatin mixture into yolks. Return yolk mixture to saucepan and blend. Cook and stir over low heat an additional 2 to 3 minutes. Remove from heat. Stir in cream cheese until combined. Stir in brandy and Creme de Cacao; cover with plastic wrap. Chill until slightly thickened. Wash beaters. Beat egg whites and cream of tartar until soft peaks form. Add remaining sugar, 1 tablespoon at a time, beating constantly until sugar is dissolved* and whites are glossy and again stand in soft peaks. Whip ½ cup cream until stiff. Gently fold cream cheese mixture and whipped cream into egg whites. Spoon about ⅓ cup souffle mixture down center of each crepe; roll up. Cover with plastic wrap; chill several hours or overnight until firm. Just before serving, whip remaining cream until stiff. Place dollop of whipped cream on each crepe; top with chocolate curls, if desired.   YIELD: 6 servings.

NOTE: Refrigerate any leftovers.

*Rub just a bit of meringue between thumb and forefinger to feel if sugar is dissolved.

Blueberry Cream Crepes

See photo at right.

Another time try blueberry pie filling to top cream-filled crepes.

12 Crepes (any size)
1 pint fresh blueberries
½ cup sugar
1 tablespoon cornstarch
¼ cup water
¼ cup light corn syrup
2 teaspoons lemon juice
2 cups dairy sour cream

Wash berries and drain. In saucepan combine sugar and cornstarch. Stir in water, corn syrup and lemon juice. Add blueberries. Cook and stir over medium heat until mixture comes to a boil and is thickened. Spoon about 2 tablespoons sour cream down center of each crepe. Roll up. Spoon blueberry sauce over to serve. YIELD: 6 servings.

Bananes Au Chocolat Crepes

Ever so easy! Bound to delight children and adults alike.

12 (5½ to 6-inch) Dessert Crepes
2 tablespoons butter, melted
2 medium-size firm bananas, cut in thin slices
¾ cup semi-sweet chocolate morsels
**   (about 4 to 5 oz.)**
Whipping cream, whipped
Toasted shredded or flaked coconut, optional

Brush crepes with melted butter. Place about 4 banana slices and 1 tablespoon chocolate morsels in center of each crepe. Fold 1 side up over filling; tuck ends in. Complete rolling with remaining side. Place seam side down on baking sheet. Bake in preheated 350°F. oven 20 to 25 minutes. Garnish with whipped cream and coconut, if desired.   YIELD: 6 servings.

Cherry Jubilee Crepes a la Creme

Light and creamy filling is an unusual twist for the flaming cherry sauce. A guaranteed success!

12 Dessert or Vanilla Crepes (any size)
1 package (3 oz.) cream cheese, softened
½ cup powdered sugar
½ cup whipping cream, whipped
1 can (1 lb.) pitted dark sweet cherries
6 slices lemon
⅓ cup granulated sugar
½ teaspoon cinnamon
⅓ cup brandy

In small mixing bowl beat cream cheese and powdered sugar together. Fold in whipped cream. Spoon 1 tablespoon cream mixture down center of each crepe. Roll up and arrange in buttered 13 x 9 x 2-inch baking pan. Bake in preheated 325°F. oven 10 minutes. Meanwhile, in saucepan heat cherries and juice with lemon slices to simmering. Pour over hot crepes and sprinkle with sugar and cinnamon. In small saucepan heat brandy. Gently pour brandy over crepes, then ignite with long-handled match. Spoon cherry sauce over crepes until flames die down. YIELD: 6 servings.

Hot Peanut Sauce

Try this over Chocolate or Cocoa Crepes filled with vanilla ice cream.

2 tablespoons sugar
2 tablespoons cornstarch
⅛ teaspoon salt
1 cup water
½ cup coarsely chopped peanuts
¼ cup Creme de Cacao

In small saucepan combine sugar, cornstarch and salt. Stir in water. Cook and stir over medium heat until mixture thickens and boils; boil and stir 1 minute. Remove from heat; stir in peanuts and liqueur.
YIELD: 1½ cups sauce.

Flaming Strawberry Crepes

See photo at right.

A spectacular dish to plan a party around.

16 (5½ to 6-inch) Crepes
1 pint fresh strawberries
⅓ cup sugar
2 cups dairy sour cream
3 tablespoons sugar
2 tablespoons orange-flavored liqueur
2 tablespoons butter
¼ cup orange-flavored liqueur

Wash and hull berries. Slice and toss with ⅓ cup sugar. Combine sour cream, 3 tablespoons sugar and 2 tablespoons liqueur. Spread 2 tablespoons sour cream over each crepe. Roll up. Cover and chill until serving time. In Crepe Suzette pan, blazer pan of chafing dish or electric skillet melt butter. Add crepes and heat, turning carefully to heat evenly. Add strawberries. In small saucepan warm ¼ cup liqueur. Pour over crepes. Ignite with long-handled match. Serve when flames die down.   YIELD: 8 servings.

Blazing Cherry Crepes

You'll need a chafing dish and a heatproof platter to present this very simple but quite spectacular dessert.

12 Crepes (any size)
1 cup dairy sour cream
⅓ cup firmly-packed brown sugar
1 can (21 oz.) cherry pie filling
¼ cup orange-flavored liqueur

Blend sour cream and brown sugar. Spread 1 tablespoon sour cream over each crepe. Roll up or fold in quarters and arrange on heatproof platter. Heat pie filling in chafing dish until bubbly. Heat liqueur in small saucepan just until warm. Gently pour liqueur over pie filling in chafing dish, then ignite with long-handled match. Spoon flaming sauce over crepes to serve.   YIELD: 4 to 6 servings.

Strawberry Patch Crepes

Very simple but also very delicious, these beautiful crepes can make your reputation as a host or hostess!

18 (5½ to 6-inch) Crepes
1 pint fresh strawberries
½ cup sugar
1 package (8 oz.) cream cheese, softened
¼ cup powdered sugar
¼ teaspoon vanilla extract

Wash and hull berries. Slice berries, then sprinkle with sugar and set aside. Beat cream cheese, powdered sugar and vanilla until light and fluffy. Gently fold in about 1 cup of the sliced berries. Spread about 1 tablespoon filling over each crepe. Roll up. Spoon remaining strawberries over crepes to serve.
YIELD: 6 servings.

Lemon Cream Crepes

Very simple, but very, very elegant. These are good prepare-ahead crepes, so you can present an impressive dessert with very little fuss.

8 Crepes (any size)
1 package (8 oz.) cream cheese, softened
1 lemon
½ cup powdered sugar
1 cup fresh orange sections or 1 can (11 oz.) mandarin orange sections, drained
½ cup chopped toasted almonds, divided

Grate peel from lemon and squeeze juice. Add peel and juice to cream cheese along with sugar and beat until light and fluffy. Gently fold in orange sections and half the almonds. Spoon about ¼ cup down center of each crepe. Roll up or fold. Sprinkle with remaining almonds.   YIELD: 4 servings.

Triple Chocolate Crepes

A Chocolate lover's delight. You could use Vanilla or Dessert Crepes in place of Chocolate Crepes.

8 Chocolate or Cocoa Crepes (any size)
1 package (6 oz.) semi-sweet chocolate
  morsels
1 cup whipping cream, whipped
3 tablespoons water

Pour ½ cup chocolate morsels into blender container and chop coarsely. Fold chopped chocolate into whipped cream and spread over crepes. Roll up. Heat remaining ½ cup chocolate morsels with water over low heat until melted. Spoon chocolate sauce over cream-filled crepes. YIELD: 8 servings.

Blueberry Crepes with Lemon Sauce

A wonderful way to enjoy fresh blueberries. In mid-winter, switch to chopped canned peaches or mandarin orange segments.

12 Dessert Crepes (any size)
½ cup sugar
2 teaspoons cornstarch
1 cup water
1 tablespoon grated lemon peel
⅓ cup lemon juice
1 pint fresh blueberries
1 cup whipping cream, whipped
2 tablespoons sugar
1 teaspoon vanilla extract

In medium saucepan combine ½ cup sugar and cornstarch. Add water, lemon peel and juice and cook and stir over medium-high heat until mixture comes to a boil and is smooth and thickened. Cool. Fold blueberries into whipped cream along with sugar and vanilla. Fill crepes with blueberry cream and roll up. Arrange on dessert plates and spoon lemon sauce over. YIELD: 6 servings.

Brown Sugar Banana Crepes

So very easy, but so very good—these crepes will become a standard in your dessert repertoire.

8 Dessert Crepes (any size)
3 tablespoons butter
3 bananas, sliced
2 tablespoons lemon juice
½ cup firmly-packed golden brown sugar
1 cup whipping cream
2 tablespoons powdered sugar

Keep crepes warm in 300°F. oven. In skillet melt butter. Add bananas, lemon juice and brown sugar. Heat, tossing gently to coat with sugar-butter mixture. Spoon bananas down center of each crepe. Fold and arrange on dessert plate. Whip cream, fold in powdered sugar and dollop on top of each crepe. YIELD: 4 servings.

Flaming Maple Crepes

Bring out your chafing dish and flame these at the table for a spectacular meal finish.

8 Dessert Crepes (any size)
6 tablespoons butter
½ cup maple-flavored pancake and
  waffle syrup
¼ cup slivered orange peel
1 tablespoon lemon juice
¼ cup brandy or 1 tablespoon lemon extract

In chafing dish or skillet melt butter. Add syrup, orange peel and lemon juice and simmer 8 to 10 minutes or until slightly thickened. Roll or fold crepes and add to simmering sauce, spooning sauce over to coat each crepe. Simmer, basting frequently, 3 to 5 minutes. In small saucepan heat brandy. Pour over crepes in chafing dish. Ignite with long-handled match. Spoon flaming sauce over crepes until flames die out. YIELD: 4 servings.

CREPES HELENE

Flaming Crepes

See photos pages 60 and 71.

Nothing's more spectacular or impressive than a flaming dish, and dessert crepes are a natural for a flaming finish. Here's how to flame crepes:

Heat a few tablespoons of brandy or liqueur (70 proof is enough to flame quite well) in a small saucepan until just warm. Don't boil. Warmed spirits ignite more easily. Slowly pour the warmed liqueur over food in a heat-proof dish or serving container. Light a long-handled match and touch to the surface of the food to ignite. If there's sauce around the crepes, use a long-handled spoon to spoon sauce over crepes until flames die down.

SOME SAFETY TIPS FOR FLAMING: Don't use more than about ¼ cup spirits. Always pour liqueur into small saucepan, never pour it right onto food, since it might ignite and flames could go right back into bottle. Keep yourself and guests a respectful distance (several feet) from pan when igniting.

Crepes Helene

See photo above.

Very easy to prepare, but very impressive to eat.

12 Dessert Crepes (any size)
1 package (3 oz.) cream cheese, softened
¾ cup dairy sour cream
2 teaspoons grated orange peel
¼ teaspoon grated lemon peel
1 cup orange marmalade

Beat cream cheese until light. Stir in sour cream, orange and lemon peel and ¼ cup of the marmalade. Spread over crepes. Roll up crepes and arrange in buttered 13 x 9 x 2-inch baking dish or shallow pan. Spread remaining marmalade over the top of crepes. Broil 6 inches from heat just until marmalade begins to bubble.   YIELD: 6 servings.

Easy Peach Pudding Crepes

Junior cooks, even those under 12, can mix up this tasty crepe filling.

16 Crepes (any size)
1 package (3½ oz.) instant vanilla pudding mix
1 teaspoon pumpkin pie spice
1 cup milk
1 jar (10 oz.) peach or apricot jam
Powdered sugar

In mixing bowl stir together pudding mix and spice. Add milk, blend well. Let stand until set. Fold in jam. Spread about 2 tablespoons pudding mixture over each crepe. Roll up. Dust with powdered sugar. YIELD: 8 servings.

Berry Crepes

See photo at right.

The photo shows straberries in the strawberry sauce, but you could also use raspberries.

12 Dessert Crepes
1 package (8 oz.) cream cheese, softened
1 package (10 oz.) frozen strawberries, thawed
⅓ cup water
⅓ cup sugar
2 tablespoons cornstarch
1 teaspoon grated lemon peel
1 pint fresh strawberries or raspberries, washed, hulled and sliced
¼ cup butter
¼ cup brandy or rum

Beat cream cheese until smooth. Spread over crepes. In blender container combine thawed strawberries, water, sugar, cornstarch, lemon peel and blend until smooth. Pour into saucepan and cook and stir over medium heat until smooth and thickened. Stir in fresh berries, butter and brandy and heat through. Spoon about 1 tablespoon berry sauce down center of each crepe. Roll up crepes and arrange on serving plates. Spoon remaining berry sauce over to serve.   YIELD: 6 servings.

Crisp Crepe Rolls

These thin, fragile cookies are a wonderful accompaniment to ice cream or fruit for dessert. They are also a great way to use less-than-perfect or leftover crepes. Just freeze extras until you have enough to prepare this way.

Crepes of any size
Butter, melted
Sugar (or cinnamon and sugar combined)

Brush one side of each crepe very lightly with melted butter and sprinkle with sugar. Roll up rather tightly into a cylinder and arrange on greased baking sheet with seam side down to hold cylinders in place. Bake in preheated 375°F. oven about 5 minutes or until crisp. Remove at once from pan and cool on rack. Carefully store in airtight container to retain crispness.

Chocolate Orange Cream Crepes

Start with Chocolate Crepes plus this simple filling and you've created a truly memorable dessert that makes enough to feed a party.

30 (5½ to 6-inch) Chocolate Crepes
3 packages (8 oz. each) cream cheese, softened
¾ cup sifted powdered sugar
¼ cup milk
2 tablespoons grated orange peel
¼ cup orange juice
Powdered sugar

In mixing bowl whip cream cheese with sugar, milk, orange peel and juice until light and fluffy. Spread each crepe with 2 level measuring tablespoonsful of cream cheese mixture. Roll up and dust with powdered sugar. YIELD: 15 servings.

Butterscotch Nut Crepes

Prepare these crepes ahead and keep them, covered, in the refrigerator until dessert time. Especially nice in Chocolate Crepes.

8 Crepes (any size)
1 package (6 oz.) butterscotch morsels
2 tablespoons corn syrup
2 tablespoons butter
2 teaspoons water
1 teaspoon freeze-dried coffee powder
¼ teaspoon salt
1 cup chopped nuts
Powdered sugar

In heavy saucepan over low heat melt butterscotch morsels, corn syrup, butter, water, coffee powder and salt, stirring until smooth. Remove from heat and stir in nuts. Cool slightly. Spread a generous tablespoon nut mixture over each crepe and roll up. Dust with powdered sugar. Serve at once or chill until serving time.   YIELD: 8 servings.

Lemony Peach Crepes

Use fresh or frozen unsweetened peaches, or 1 pint straw- or raspberries.

12 Vanilla Crepes (any size)
2 cups diced fresh peaches, nectarines, pears or plums
¼ cup sugar
2 teaspoons vanilla extract
½ cup butter
1½ cups sugar
3 eggs
3 egg yolks
1½ teaspoons grated lemon peel
½ cup lemon juice
⅛ teaspoon salt
1 tablespoon vanilla extract

Sprinkle peaches with ½ cup sugar and 2 teaspoons vanilla and set aside. In heavy saucepan melt butter, stir in 1½ cups sugar. Beat eggs and yolks and stir into sugar-butter mixture, then blend in lemon peel, juice and salt. Cook and stir over low heat until mixture is smooth and thickened. Remove from heat, stir in 1 tablespoon vanilla. Cool. Stir in peaches. Spoon 2 tablespoons filling down center of each crepe. Roll up and arrange 2 crepes on each dessert plate. Spoon remaining peach sauce over.   YIELD: 6 servings.

Date Nut Crepes

Citrus juices give this date nut mixture a delicious tang. Serve them hot or cooled.

12 Dessert Crepes (any size)
1 package (8 oz.) diced dates
1 cup sugar
¼ cup water
1 can (15¼ oz.) crushed pineapple, drained
¼ cup orange juice
1½ teaspoons grated lemon peel
1 tablespoon lemon juice
½ cup chopped walnuts or pecans
Whipping cream, whipped

In large saucepan combine dates, sugar, water and pineapple. Cook and stir over medium-high heat until mixture boils and is thickened. Add orange juice, lemon peel and lemon juice; cook and stir an additional 5 minutes. Remove from heat. Stir in walnuts. Spoon about 3 tablespoons mixture down center of each crepe. Roll up. Dollop with whipped cream. YIELD: 6 servings.

Apricot Almond Crepes

Invite guests for after-theater dessert and then wow them with this creation.

12 Vanilla Crepes (any size)
1 package (8 oz.) cream cheese, softened
¼ cup sugar
2 teaspoons vanilla extract
1 teaspoon grated lemon peel
1½ tablespoons butter, melted
⅔ cup apricot jam
⅓ cup orange juice
2 tablespoons butter
1 tablespoon vanilla extract
¼ cup toasted slivered almonds

In mixing bowl beat cream cheese, sugar, 2 teaspoons vanilla and lemon peel until light and fluffy. Spread cheese mixture over all crepes. Fold two opposite sides of crepe together, then roll up from unfolded side. Arrange in buttered 13 x 9 x 2-inch baking pan and brush with melted butter. Heat in preheated 350°F. oven while preparing sauce. In small saucepan heat jam, orange juice, 2 tablespoons butter and vanilla until smooth. Spoon over hot crepes and sprinkle with almonds to serve.   YIELD: 6 servings.

Raspberry Sauced Cheese Crepes

Delicious with the cheese filling here, the raspberry sauce is also tasty on ice cream or pudding-filled crepes.

12 Dessert Crepes (any size)
1 package (10 oz.) frozen raspberries
Water
2 tablespoons sugar
2 tablespoons cornstarch
⅓ cup maple syrup
1 package (8 oz.) cream cheese, softened
¼ cup milk

Drain raspberries, reserving syrup; set aside. Add water to syrup to make ⅔ cup; set aside. In saucepan combine sugar and cornstarch. Stir in reserved raspberry liquid. Bring to a boil, stirring constantly; boil and stir 1 minute. Stir in maple syrup and reserved raspberries. Keep warm while preparing filling. Beat cream cheese with milk until smooth and light. Spoon about 1½ tablespoons cheese mixture down center of each crepe. Roll up. Top each crepe with about 2 tablespoons warm raspberry sauce.   YIELD: 4 to 6 servings.

Plum Dumpling Crepes

These make a delightful dessert or a marvelous main dish accompaniment, especially for roast duckling. Double the recipe for hearty appetites.

12 Dessert Crepes (any size)
12 small fresh plums
12 sugar cubes or 2 tablespoons sugar,
**   divided**
¾ cup fine dry bread crumbs
3 tablespoons butter, melted

Remove pits from plums, being careful to keep them whole. Replace each pit with a sugar cube or ½ teaspoon sugar. Place a plum in the center of each crepe. Fold 1 side up over plum; tuck ends in. Complete rolling with remaining side. Combine bread crumbs and butter. Carefully roll each crepe in buttered crumbs. Place on baking sheet. Bake in preheated 350°F. oven 15 to 20 minutes. YIELD: 6 servings.

Fruit Melange Crepes

The fresh fruits in this recipe may be varied to your taste. Try fresh blueberries or raspberries in place of the strawberries. If you prefer, the crepes may be topped with sour cream and brown sugar or with toasted flaked coconut.

12 Dessert Crepes (any size)
1 pint strawberries, hulled and sliced
1½ tablespoons granulated sugar
1 can (8¼ oz.) crushed pineapple with syrup
1 tablespoon butter
¼ teaspoon cinnamon
1 banana, thinly sliced
1 teaspoon lemon juice
Powdered sugar

Sprinkle strawberries with granulated sugar; set aside. In saucepan combine pineapple with syrup, butter and cinnamon. Bring to a boil, stirring constantly. Stir in reserved strawberries, banana slices and lemon juice. Spoon about ¼ cup fruit mixture down center of each crepe. Roll up. Dust with powdered sugar.   YIELD: 6 servings.

Hungarian Dessert Crepes

Ever so simple with ingredients on hand. A delightful reward for little effort.

12 Dessert Crepes (any size)
1½ cups preserves (your favorite flavor)
¾ cup chopped almonds
Powdered sugar

Spread each crepe with 2 tablespoons preserves. Sprinkle evenly with 1 tablespoon almonds. Fold into quarters. Arrange on greased baking sheet. Dust with powdered sugar. Bake in preheated 375°F. oven 15 minutes.   YIELD: 4 to 6 servings.

CREATE YOUR OWN CREPES

After you've tried some recipes from each of the other sections, you may feel adept enough to begin mixing up your own crepe fillings. The suggestions that follow are ideas of combinations you might like to try. Perhaps your family has some very special favorites that could go into a crepe. Why not?

Crepe Toppers

Sprinkle filled crepes with buttered bread crumbs before baking or broiling for a special finishing touch. Or crumble salad croutons over crepes and drizzle with melted butter. Cracker, potato chip or other snack food crumbs also make a nice finish to crepes.

Shredded cheese tops almost any main dish crepe to perfection. Or try just a dusting of grated Parmesan cheese. Run crepes under broiler until just lightly browned.

Simple Sauces

Spoon sauce over filled crepes or use some sauce in the filling and some on the top. Many marvelous sauce ideas start with a can of condensed soup. Mushroom sauce, for example, can come from a can of cream of mushroom soup mixed with the contents (liquid too) of a 4-ounce can of sliced mushrooms.

Make a mock Hollandaise by stirring ¼ cup mayonnaise and 2 tablespoons lemon juice into a can of cream of chicken soup. Or use sour cream in place of mayonnaise. A great cover for fish or poultry filled crepes.

Wine sauce starts with any condensed cream soup and ¼ cup sherry or white wine. You can add a tablespoon or two of grated Parmesan or shredded Swiss cheese for extra richness and tang.

If you're using any canned food, save about ¼ cup of the liquid to mix with canned soup for a special sauce. Canned shrimp or salmon liquid flavors cream of shrimp or cream of asparagus soup; or liquid from frozen thawed crab could go into cream of mushroom or cream of onion soup.

Simple Stroganoff sauce starts with cream of onion soup and ends with ¼ to ½ cup of dairy sour cream.

Soup and salad dressing mixes (dry) can flavor sauces and fillings. Stir half a package into a cup of dairy sour cream, or ½ cup sour cream and ½ cup mayonnaise. Thin with a little lemon juice, wine, vinegar or milk. Use half this mixture to bind filling ingredients and spoon the remainder over the filled crepes.

Packaged sauce mixes can be the inspiration for many a crepe topper. Try spaghetti sauce mix (prepared as package directs) over crepes filled with cottage cheese, or ground beef. Stir up sweet sour sauce mix to go over turkey or tuna crepes. Hollandaise, Stroganoff and taco sauces are other possibilities.

Fast and Fancy Fillings

That cup or so of pieces left from Sunday's roast can make a great encore as a crepe filling. Cut the meat in small dice size pieces and mix with canned soup, sour cream, leftover gravy, prepared sauce from a mix; add some chopped onion, celery green pepper or other vegetable, season with inspiration and roll it all up in a crepe.

On the day you clean the refrigerator, plan on crepes for supper. Tag ends of almost anything, as long as they are still fresh and flavorful, can make Crepes Surprise. How about ends and pieces of leftover cheese, ground or shredded, mixed with mayonnaise, some grated onion and bacon pieces, then wrapped in crepes and deep-fried? Or three kinds of vegetables, stirred into a cup of cream sauce or leftover gravy, rolled up in Parmesan Crepes and broiled? Even leftover stew, with meat chunks cut down to size (vegetables as well) can reappear in a new guise as Crepes Francaise.

(You'll discover that half the fun of creating your own crepes is coming up with names for them.)

Everyday common food favorites become a little different when wrapped in a crepe. Try ham salad with Cheddar cheese cubes in Herbed Crepes; egg salad with green pepper and chopped olives in Parmesan Crepes; tuna salad with chopped pimiento-stuffed green olives in Basic Crepes.

Instead of sandwiching food combinations, crepe them. Peanut butter and jelly makes a great crepe. Thin-sliced ham and cheese rolls up in dill or carraway-flavored crepes to a supreme treat. Reuben filling in crepes—a masterpiece!

Spread deviled ham or chicken spread over Parmesan Crepes, sprinkle with some chopped celery or green pepper, some shredded Swiss or Cheddar cheese. Roll up and heat.

Your canned food shelf can supply the basis of many a crepe delight. Canned chicken ala king in crepes, for example. Or brown some ground beef, stir in a can of chili or some refried beans and fill Corn Meal Crepes.

Casserole combinations make tasty crepe fillings. Just fix up your favorite combination, leaving out the rice or noodle extenders, then spoon into crepes or stack between crepes to form a cake or gateau.

Turkey leftovers, or plannedovers, are the start of many a special crepe. Cubed cooked turkey plus cream of chicken soup, sherry, mushrooms and a little sour cream makes a filling any chef would envy. Or blend cream cheese with drained cranberry orange relish and turkey cubes and serve in crepes, unheated.

Turkey plus bottled or canned sweet sour sauce, with pineapple chunks, green pepper squares and sliced water chestnuts is easier than pie. Or toss turkey cubes with cream of asparagus soup to spoon over crepes wrapped around asparagus spears. Finish off with a sprinkling of Swiss or Parmesan cheese.

Roast beef needn't go into hash when crepes are waiting. That roast beef can become Stroganoff. Or stir it with spaghetti or tomato sauce, roll up in crepes and top with slices or shreds of Mozzarella cheese. Mix a cup or two of dairy sour cream with dry onion soup mix, then add leftover beef, lamb or pork cubes and use to fill crepes.

Brown some pork sausage, drain well and then stir in applesauce, a dash of cinnamon and just a drizzle of maple syrup. Roll up in crepes and spoon more applesauce over the top.

Canned luncheon meat waits on your shelf to go into crepes. Try cubes with applesauce or sour cream or sweet sour sauce. Or try slices or chunks of hot dogs or tiny Vienna sausages in applesauce, drained crushed pineapple or apple pie filling.

Even something as effortless as scrambled eggs makes a terrific crepe filling. Scramble the eggs Denver-style, with ham, green pepper and onion, then sauce filled crepes with tomato or spaghetti sauce. Or scramble egg with cubes of cream cheese and some chopped fresh herbs, to roll up in Parmesan or Herb Crepes. Try stirring half a can of asparagus soup and some cut canned asparagus into scrambled eggs. Mix the remaining soup with a tablespoon each of mayonnaise and lemon juice and spoon over top.

Quiche, that impressive-sounding and oh-so-easy to fix cheese-egg custard is a natural to bake in small crepes lining muffin tins. Do be sure to use crepes without any holes, so filling won't leak. Crepe Quiche combinations are limitless. For 12 crepe cups try: 4 eggs, a can of tomato soup and 2 cups of cubed process American cheese, with instant onion, salt and pepper. Or 4 to 6 eggs, a tall can of evaporated milk, a package of onion soup mix and some Parmesan cheese.

Creamed eggs can be the beginning of several superb crepe fillings. To the simple mixture of cream sauce (2 tablespoons butter, 2 tablespoons flour, ½ teaspoon salt, dash pepper and 1 cup milk or cream) add 6 chopped hard-cooked eggs. Then try curry powder, chopped chives and parsley, chopped fresh dill or rosemary, bacon bits, minced leftover vegetables or meats. Spoon it all into crepes, roll up, heat and enjoy.

Saute some chicken livers, cut in bite-sized pieces and then mix with spaghetti sauce. Spoon into crepes and you've Crepes Caruso. Stir livers into sour cream or Stroganoff sauce and you've a different dish.

Chop some sauerkraut and mix with cubed leftover roast pork, chicken, turkey or beef, or some browned sausage or ground beef. Then add a little cream cheese or sour cream or some shredded Swiss cheese to form a rich sauce as the filling bakes in crepes.

Mix cubed cooked chicken with a package of cooked and drained frozen chopped spinach and some drained canned mushrooms. Stir in a little cream cheese to richen it all up and try in Parmesan Crepes.

Bottled barbecue sauce plus cubed cold cooked meat equals savory crepes.

For a California-style crepe, mix chicken cubes with tomato chunks, avocado cubes and mayonnaise and serve in Corn Meal Crepes.

Crepe Dippers are great bases for caviar or sardines, even chunks of creamed herring.

A crepe can be the beginning of a rolled pizza. Spread Corn Meal or Parmesan Crepes with canned pizza sauce, scatter with mushrooms, peppers, pepperoni bits or anchovies, roll up. Top with more pizza sauce, Mozzarella cheese.

Cottage cheese goes in blintzes and rolled or quarter-folded crepes too. Stir some mixed dried herbs into cottage cheese. Or some drained crushed pineapple.

Packaged entrees from your freezer—such as creamed chicken, barbecued beef, beef stroganoff—taste more like homemade if you serve them in crepes. Add one of the toppers suggested at the beginning of this section, and you've made a specialty of your house.

Desserts

Start with ice cream wrapped in a crepe and you've opened the door to hundreds of dessert possibilities. Chocolate sauce, fudge sauce, caramel sauce, maple syrup with pecans, shaved chocolate and coffee liqueur, fresh fruits, etc., etc., etc.

Pick up a jar of jam, jelly or preserves, any flavor you choose. Stir in 2 tablespoons lemon juice, wine or liqueur and heat. Spoon over crepes, quarter-fold or roll up and run under the broiler for just a minute or two. Just like in France. Flame them, if you wish.

Packaged or canned puddings stir up into super crepe fillings. Add toasted almonds, buttered pecans, sugared walnuts, chocolate chips, toasted coconut if you wish.

Whip some cream, prepare packaged dessert topping mix or thaw frozen whipped topping. Stir in crushed peppermint candies, shaved chocolate or chocolate shot, liqueur, cocoa, coconut, nuts, grated orange peel or lime peel. Spoon into crepes.

Canned pie filling is a great crepe stuffer all by itself. Or stir in a tablespoon of liqueur, wine or lemon juice; a half teaspoon of cinnamon, nutmeg, mace, ginger or allspice; half a cup of chopped nuts or toasted coconut. Sprinkle some Cheddar cheese over crepes full of apple pie filling; spoon lemon or custard sauce over other fruit fillings or mincemeat.

Make up pie filling mixes as label directs for meringue pies. Spoon filling into crepes, then top with meringue and brown in 350°F. oven.

Drain canned fruit, reserving syrup. Blend 1 tablespoon cornstarch and 1 tablespoon sugar in a saucepan, then add a cup of syrup (or syrup plus water) and cook and stir until mixture comes to a boil and is smooth and thickened. Stir in lemon juice and peel, vanilla or a spice of your choice, then drained fruit. Heat through to spoon over or in Dessert Crepes.

Make blintzes from cottage or Ricotta cheese moistened with a dab of sour cream and flavored with drained crushed pineapple, mixed candied fruit, chopped dates or raisins, chopped nuts, chopped chocolate or crushed peppermint candy.

Whip cream cheese with milk or orange or lemon juice until fluffy, then spread over or spoon in crepes. Top with chocolate sauce, dark sweet cherries and syrup, quick-thaw frozen cherries or strawberries, raspberry preserves, crème de menthe or fruit-flavored syrups.

Frozen fruit salad mixtures—the ones with cream cheese, mayonnaise, canned drained fruit cocktail and maraschino cherries—are natural crepe fillings. Serve cold from the refrigerator, or frosty from the freezer.

You can make a parfait crepe by spreading 4 crepes with whipped topping or cream, 4 with fruit, preserves or sundae sauce and then stacking to form a cake. Cut wedges to serve.

Packaged dessert mixes made to be chilled in dessert glasses were also made to be chilled in crepes. Mix up chocolate, strawberry and vanilla flavors and dollop a spoonful of each in the center of crepes for Crepes Neapolitan.

Drain canned pears or peaches, thicken sauce with a little cornstarch and then stir in minced candied ginger and a tablespoon of butter to spoon over quarter-folded Dessert Crepes made with macaroon crumbs.

Soak mixed dried fruits, then chop and stir into Danish dessert prepared from a mix. Raspberries or strawberries, folded in Danish dessert along with tiny cubes of cream cheese, make another marvelous dessert.

Combine honey and soft butter with a little cinnamon and spread over several crepes. Sprinkle each crepe generously with chopped nuts, then stack. Serve as is, or heat, then cut wedges to serve topped with whipped cream.

Spread crepes with lemon curd or orange marmalade and quarter fold. Prepare custard sauce and chill before spooning over. Toasted almonds add the finishing touch.

Stack crepes with mincemeat in between and decorate top with hard sauce or rum sauce.

Slice fresh apples or pears and saute in butter. Sprinkle with brown sugar and mace and cook until soft. Spoon into crepes and then top with ice cream.

Use cookie or cake crumbs to add a finishing touch to baked sweet crepes. Brush filled crepes with melted butter, then with crumbs and brown in oven or broiler.

Veloute Sauce

A classic French sauce which is just as tasty on vegetables as it is on meats, poultry or seafood. Use as the beginning of many create your own specials.

2 tablespoons butter
2 tablespoons flour
¼ teaspoon salt
⅛ teaspoon pepper
⅛ teaspoon nutmeg
1 cup chicken broth
½ cup light cream or half and half

Melt butter; blend in flour and seasonings. Cook and stir over medium heat until smooth and bubbly. Stir in broth and cream. Cook and stir until mixture boils and is smooth and thickened.   YIELD: about 1½ cups.

Yogurt Crepe Batter

A delightfully delicate flavor enhancer for crepes. Yogurt makes a butterless batter.

3 eggs
¾ cup plain yogurt
¼ cup water
1 cup all-purpose flour
¼ teaspoon salt

BLENDER METHOD: Combine all ingredients in blender container; blend about 1 minute. Scrape down sides of blender container with rubber spatula. Blend until smooth, about 30 additional seconds.

MIXER, ROTARY BEATER OR WHISK METHOD: Combine eggs, yogurt and water in mixing bowl; beat until combined. Add flour and salt; beat until smooth.

Refrigerate batter 1 hour.

YIELD: About 2 cups batter.

Dieter's Crepe Batter

You may need to oil or butter the pan occasionally between these crepes as they are almost fat-free. Make them more exciting by adding herbs.

3 eggs
1 cup water
¾ cup all-purpose flour
¼ cup nonfat dry milk
¼ teaspoon salt

BLENDER: METHOD: Combine all ingredients in blender container; blend about 1 minute. Scrape down sides of blender container with rubber spatula. Blend until smooth, about 30 additional seconds.

MIXER, ROTARY BEATER OR WHISK METHOD: Combine eggs and water in mixing bowl; beat until combined. Add flour, dry milk and salt; beat until smooth.

Refrigerate batter 1 hour.

YIELD: About 2¼ cups batter.

INDEX